School Of Hard Knocks

Life Lessons for the Block
From Proverbs 13

By

Blanton P. Hardy

School Of Hard Knocks
Life Lessons for the Block From Proverbs 13
Vol I
Blanton Pierre Hardy

Published By Parables
November, 2019

Copyright © Blanton Pierre Hardy 2015

All rights reserved. No part of this book may be used or reproduced by any means, graphic, electronic or mechanical, including photocopying, recording or taping or by any information storage retrieval system without the written permission of the publisher except in the case of brief quotations embodied in critical articles and reviews.

This novel is a work of fiction. Characters, places and incidents either are the product of the author's imagination or are used fictitiously. Any resemblance to actual events, locales, organizations or persons living or dead is entirely coincidental.

Because of the dynamic nature of the Internet, any web addresses or links contained in this book may have changed since publication and may no longer valid. The views expressed in this work are solely those of the author and do not necessarily reflect the views of the publisher, and the publisher hereby disclaims any responsibility for them.

Any people depicted in stock imagery provided by Stock Photos for Free are models, and such images are being used for illustrative purposes only.

Certain stock imagery © Stock Photos for Free

Cover Photo Provided by: Green View Photography
Copyright © Sue Green
www.Greenview.smugmug.com
www.greenviewphoto.etsy.com

Library of Congress Control Number: 2013956572

Printed in the United States of America

Readers should be aware that Internet Web sites offered as citations and/or sources for further information may have been changed or disappeared between the time this was written and the time it is read.

All scripture is taken from the HOLY BIBLE, KING JAMES VERSION.

Inspirational thoughts for the book are taken from the Matthew Henry Commentary.

School Of Hard Knocks

Life Lessons for the Block From Proverbs 13
Volume 1
Blanton P. Hardy

Edited By Christy Smith

DEDICATION

In dedication to Christ and Carolyn, my mom and those family and friends and those publishers and editors who inspired me along the way.

Introduction

Analysis of The Book Of Proverbs

ON THE BLOCK

About The Author

The lessons:

1. A wise son heareth his father's instruction: but a scorner heareth not rebuke.

2. A man shall eat good by the fruit of his mouth: but the soul of the transgressors shall eat violence.

3. He that keepeth his mouth keepeth his life: but he that openeth wide his lips shall have destruction.

4. The soul of the sluggard desireth, and hath nothing: but the soul of the diligent shall be made fat.

5. A righteous man hateth lying: but a

wicked man is loathsome, and cometh to shame.

6. Righteousness keepeth him that is upright in the way: but wickedness overthroweth the sinner.

7. There is that maketh himself rich, yet hath nothing: there is that maketh himself poor, yet hath great riches.

8. The ransom of a man's life are his riches: but the poor heareth not rebuke.

9. The light of the righteous rejoiceth: but the lamp of the wicked shall be put out.

10. Only by pride cometh contention: but with the well advised is wisdom.

11. Wealth gotten by vanity shall be diminished: but he that gathereth by labour shall increase.

12. Hope deferred maketh the heart sick: but when the desire cometh, it is a tree of life.

13. Whoso despiseth the word shall be destroyed: but he that feareth the commandment shall be rewarded.

14. The law of the wise is a fountain of life, to depart from the snares of death.

15. Good understanding giveth favour: but the way of transgressors is hard.

16. Every prudent man dealeth with knowledge: but a fool layeth open his folly.

17. A wicked messenger falleth into mischief: but a faithful ambassador is health.

18. Poverty and shame shall be to him that refuseth instruction: but he that regardeth reproof shall be honoured.

19. The desire accomplished is sweet to the soul: but it is abomination to fools to depart from evil.

20. He that walketh with wise men shall be wise: but a companion of fools shall be destroyed.

21. Evil pursueth sinners: but to the righteous good shall be repayed.

22. A good man leaveth an inheritance to his children's children: and the wealth of the sinner is laid up for the just.

23. Much food is in the tillage of the poor: but there is that is destroyed for want of judgment.

24. He that spareth his rod hateth his son: but he that loveth him chasteneth him betimes.

25. The righteous eateth to the satisfying of his soul: but the belly of the wicked shall want.

School Of Hard Knocks Vol I

Introduction

It is very obvious today that there are a variety of people giving a variety of opinions and advice. Advice on what to wear, advice on how to speak to a woman/man, advice on how to keep your finances in check, or how to keep your marriage or family in line. So there are a variety of opinions and advice on what things you should and should not do in your life.

Now some advice given is fruitful and productive and some advice is not. We have taken the advice of family or friends and have taken the right path, and sometimes we have taken their advice which led to disastrous consequences. It is said the only thing you really own and possess in this world are your thoughts and your actions, both of which will lead you into a prosperous life, or one that leads into a dead end road. So in this society, the best question that would be to ask is, where are the wisdom and wise words being spoken?

Proverbs is what is known in the Bible the "consciousness of the Word of God. While the whole Bible matures, structures and disciplines the spirit as well as conscious, Proverbs is meant specifically to focus on the conscious of man, or the right way and wrong way to do things. In this society, we have so many things directing our steps other than God. Proverbs focuses on how you can live at peace with God and man.

Someone has said that when God deals with us that we are a WIP (Work-In-Progress) but then someone came in front of that and said that we are actually a MIP (Masterpiece-In-Progress). When God deals with us, He deals with creating masterpieces. I myself included, as I am writing this, am a work-in-progress working day by day to keep these simple truths of God that sometimes I triumph and sometime I fail. God never lets His sheep out of His hand. God's wisdom is His refining tools to create something in us that we may look like Him.

My prayer is that you will take from this book the wisdom necessary for you to survive and know how to make the right decision in any situation; not only on the street or block, but also in the world in general and in the lives of your family and your friends. Let God's wisdom mature not only you but those around you.

The Analysis of the Book Of Proverbs

The book of Proverbs was written by one of the wisest men in Israel at the time; that man was King Solomon. He reigned as king of Israel from 970 - 930 BCE. One of the wisest men in the Israel province, he ruled with the wisdom granted by the God of Israel. People came from miles around to hear his wisdom. Even the Queen of Sheba whose name was Queen Makeda came to hear the wisdom of this great man. However, because of his many wives that worshiped other gods, King Solomon started to set up idols in Jerusalem, therefore in a sense turning his back on God and worshiping other idols. Therefore God took His hand of protection away from King Solomon and his empire fell because as said by scripture, he forgot his first love, which was God.

Of course, this is not the first time that wise words were used to build or govern a kingdom. Going back to 2160-2686 A.D., we see the words of The Instructions of Kagem-ni and The Instructions of Prince Hor-dedef, two classic works in wisdom literature. There was one item that wisdom literature like this was missing, a knowledge of the supremacy of God. Solomon states in the first chapter of Proverbs 1:7 "The fear of the Lord is the beginning of knowledge; but fools despise wisdom and instruction." So there was, of course, knowledge before the time of Solomon put in a proverbial form, however none of it revealed the source of the knowledge. Solomon was bold enough to say that true wisdom and instruction comes from God and those who possess Godly knowledge and wisdom.

Basically, the lessons that we learn here in a nutshell are very simple. Any knowledge that is not based on the foundation of God will fall. Just as Solomon's temple did when he made the decision to allow idols into their midst. As we delve into this book, you will see examples of this in action.

ON THE BLOCK

This book in general can be used by anyone as the Word of God itself can be used by all mankind and is not centered toward a certain group because the Word of God is for all men in all circumstances and situations, however, in this book, special attention is focused on how to use wisdom on our own block and in our community, not to mention also dealing on street knowledge level and how to deal with certain situations not only on the street but also in life in general.

"The block" as we would call it consists of our community. Every community has a block or corner and every community has certain rules to follow if you want to survive. To learn how to survive in your own surroundings is the basics of survival, period. If you don't know how to survive in just common life or in your own block as far as natural issues that may happen around your own community, then you will be hard-pressed when it comes to surviving in the real world.

There was a terminology a few years ago during the 1990's amongst the Hip Hop and in the urban community that was called "Droppin Jewels." which simply meant that a certain person is giving bits of wisdom he/she can use in life. This saying was formed from different sources but mostly striving and maintaining and striving towards the virtues and principles of knowledge, wisdom, understanding, freedom, justice, equality, food, clothing, shelter, love, peace and happiness. Thus the saying "Droppin Jewels" was born because these were jewels that people on the street lived by and strived for.

Believe it or not, this saying, as urban as it was, the Bible teaches on the same exact things and how to achieve them through the true knowledge of God, which is the Bible. Scripture tells us in Proverbs 8:11 "For wisdom is better than rubies; and all the things that may be desired are not to be compared to it." Also Proverbs 3:15 states, "She (wisdom) is more precious than rubies: and all the things thou canst desire are not to be compared unto her." and finally Proverbs 20:15 "There is gold, and a multitude of rubies: but the lips of knowledge are a precious jewel." Each time that knowledge is referred to, especially in Proverbs 20:15, it is referred to as a jewel. This book is basically about giving you the true jewels of God which come out of His Word. No other wisdom compares to His. These are the true jewels of God that you can use for everyday life and everyday experiences in life. However, as I have said, please don't misunderstand. The Word of God is meant not only for the person on the street, it is written for ALL men and ALL women because as scripture says all men need to be saved. (2 Peter 3:9).

In this book, we will be looking at Proverbs 13, or what I call God's School Of Hard Knocks. Everything you need to learn about how to just survive life in general on a daily basis is given in this short primer. Do not think however this is a supplement for the WHOLE Bible;

these scriptures in particular detail on why things happen, and how they should happen if wisdom is applied. My greatest prayer and hope is that these principles will be utilized not only to address any problem or issue that happens on street level but also the larger society and world that we inhabit. So without further ado (and talk), let's get on with our study into the book of Proverbs.

Lesson 1:

A wise son heareth his father's instruction: but a scorner heareth not rebuke.

(Proverbs 13:1)

If it could be said there is one crisis in our world today that would be a lack of true fatherhood. Fathers play an essential role in the maturation of sons and daughters. They are not only the breadwinners of the family, but also the law and the maturity instructor in the family. Their main essential role of a father is to lay down the law and to strengthen attributes in the child that help prepare him/her for later life. As said once by a young man once, "In a family, there should be two figures of the family, the father, and the mother. The father is there to give guidance and discipline and brings discipline and self-reliance out of a person. The mother is there for love and comfort and to build up the love within a child. If any of these elements are missing out of a family, then that person will lack in that area of life." You can always tell most of the time which figure of the family is missing from an individual's life because of the way the individual treats and acts toward other people. As the key scripture says a scorner heareth not a father's rebuke. Rebuke builds discipline within a person. So if a person is always spewing and talking about, "I'm going to do things my way!!" or "Nobody is going to tell me what to do!" Then as scripture says that area of discipline is lacking because discipline puts a person in line with the fact, you *cannot* do what you want to do. Not only for the fact that this person says so, but because later on in life whether it be in a job or a marriage, without that discipline and toughness whatever endeavor you take will fail or at least be a wasted effort on what God wanted that person to do for him.

The scripture tells us that scorners shall follow this path. To scorn means to hold in contempt or disdain. It really means not to even hear the advice of the father. Some of the most well-known and perverse people and celebrities nowadays when you look into their lives, the first thing that comes up is the fact his/her home life as a young boy/girl was always in turmoil. Home is the basis for all instruction. If the environment is bad, then that person will ninety percent of the time turn out bad in some area or another especially in moral or proper behavior, simply because the environment in that household corrupting the moral upbringing of the child.

However, this does not only have to happen in bad households but also in good ones without God's Word and instruction in that household. A side note, the excuse is usually used, "I act this way because I didn't have a father growing up." While in today's society the reality is the human father is M.I.A. from the family, it needs to be known in a family there is an order. The children listen to the mother, the mother listens to the father and the father

listens to God and relays the message back to the mother; then the mother relays the message back to the children.
even though you are to listen and obey your father's instructions, there is an ultimate father that you are to pay strict attention to, *even in some cases over your physical father*. That father is God and Jesus Christ in particular. If the human father is gone out of the family you still have the surrogate father of heaven and earth whose attention you should be attending to already.

Pray for your family daily that they will teach you the right way and path of righteousness according to Christ Jesus, and also that you will be as James 1:19 "Able to be swift to hear, slow to speak, slow to wrath."

WISDOM for the block:

Whether it be a father in the home or a father in heaven, without the discipline and tutelage of a father, surviving in the streets or in this world will be impossible.

Prayer: God change our rebellious and revengeful hearts back to you. Let us hear sound wisdom and instruction not only from you but from the fathers that you have put on this earth to guide us. Thank you God for your wisdom and thank you for not letting us fall into the hands and the mindset of the scornful.

In the strong name of Jesus, we pray.

Amen.

Lesson 2:

A man shall eat good by the fruit of his mouth: but the soul of the transgressors shall eat violence.

(Proverbs 13:2)

I have always said and always been a big believer in the fact that your values will lead you to wherever you want to go, whether they be good or whether they be bad. If you hold Godly or righteous values, then those values will lead you toward Godly things; if you hold or have evil values, they will lead you toward evil things or situations and also ultimately an evil destination and fate. When you look on television and see young men and women selling drugs or doing some illegal activity, the response that is usually given to these acts by the ones committing the crimes is usually, "Aiyyo man, I gotta eat!!" or "Aiyyo man, I gotta provide for my family somehow." Or the newest one nowadays, "Aiyyo man, I gotta feed my kids man!" The only way to really get paid or really get some type of income in most environments and situations is to rob, kill, and steal for a dollar because the pressure is on to not starve either their family members or themselves.

However, that is just the problem, the pressure. The pressure of trying to make things work when there seems to be no way out or no way to make things work. How does a person not rob, kill, or steal to get what they need to survive? Two words...Trust God!

One of the main jobs of the devil is to make a person believe and put an obstacle in front of an individual so that the only way to do things or to get over this obstacle would be to do something illegal or even immoral. God is the direct opposite of the devil himself. He is the author and prince of all peace. The devil's job is to rob, kill, and destroy in that order. Once you give in to the devil, he will rob you of your peace, then kill your hopes and dreams, and then once he is finished with you he will ultimately destroy your very life. How does this connect on to our scripture? That's very simple.

When you steal or disrespect another person, you just stole that person's respect or property. Now who is to say that person will not take their revenge out on you for doing that? In the street, it is called the code or cycle or respect, orr to term it scripturally, an eye for an eye and a tooth for a tooth. If you happen to steal someone's car, then ninety percent of the time you have just put yourself in a position to be arrested by the police, or God forbid, if that person you stole the car from ever sees you on the street, you are now in a position to be shot by that person that you stole from. Sounds ridiculous? There was a time when rappers were wearing and really still wearing all these fancy jewels. (We call them Ice or Bling Bling, by the way) But then what started occurring was people were getting those exact same jewels stolen that they were showing off. This was a trend started called Emcee Jacking. Because people were naive enough to think that you could walk around in the worst neighborhoods with numerous articles of jewelry on and nothing would become of it. So the old saying goes, What goes around comes around. You steal from me, I steal your life. How can a person make and provide for themselves and their families without trying to rob, kill, and steal which is what the devil wants?

The first thing you have to know is that God is a provider. King David, one of the most powerful kings in Israel, said in Psalms 37:25: "I have been young, and now am old; yet have I not seen the righteous forsaken, nor his seed begging bread." That means that God will provide all your needs according to HIS riches and glory and not YOURS. Basically, there are two things that you have to realize. Without Jesus, your plans will go nowhere. I know that may seem like the biggest falsehood right now because it seems as if all the evil men are rich and the good are always in poverty. Where is the true wealth? First off, God did not promise that you would be wealthy. He said he will provide all your NEEDS, not WANTS, but NEEDS, according to HIS riches and glory. Realize that the only way to get true prosperity is to be connected to Jesus. Jesus made it very plain in John chapter 15:7 "If ye abide in me, and my words abide in you, ye shall ask what ye will, and it shall be done unto you." Which means whatever you ask in Jesus' name, he will give it to you! Hold on, don't start jumping up and down just yet. If we go a few scriptures down there is a condition. If we look at John chapter 15:14, he tells us that to get this connection you must be a friend of Jesus. To be a friend of Jesus, according to John chapter 15:14 "If ye do whatsoever I command you." You will not be able to get anything if you do not obey Jesus. God's will is not to let anyone perish or starve, but the way that you choose is the way that will lead you down that road of hardship. You must stay connected to Jesus and His life and teachings to get anything in life.

The second thing that has to be realized is that our key scripture says that a man shall eat by the fruit of his mouth. I hear so many people say "There are no job opportunities man!" There is one thing that needs to be said in respect of that, if you can't find an opportunity....make one! When I hear that there are no opportunities in certain communities, I wonder what happened to the young men who wanted to be astronauts; what happened to the young men who wanted to be firemen; what happened to the young men who wanted to be doctors? Not taking away from it, but not all people are cut out to be a rap emcee or shoot a ball through a hoop. God put in every individual a gift and a talent to shine for His glory.

Pray what it is that God wants to use you for. Use that and you will get paid guaranteed!

Scripture tells us in Ecclesiastes 9:10: "Whatsoever thy hand findeth to do, do it with thy might;" Whatever God has blessed you with, use that to get your money and more importantly to bring someone to the realization that all thing are possible through Christ Jesus.

In essence, you don't have to rob, steal, or kill anymore to have some change in your pocket. Use your talents to get paid. Because the other road is a road that leads to a cardboard box six feet under. Please believe me on this.

WISDOM for the block:

To use the talents that God has given you is more fulfilling than anything you can imagine, but to rob, kill and destroy just leads you to a long prison sentence or a quick death.

Prayer: God give us wisdom to put our hand to the plow and never look back. Help us be successful not only in this life but also for how you want us to use our talents to show your love and impact someone's life for the better.

In the majestic name of Jesus, we pray.

Amen.

Lesson 3:

He that keepeth his mouth keepeth his life but he that openeth wide his lips shall have destruction.

(Proverbs 13:3)

Years ago, there was a popular saying which went, loose lips sinks ships, which demonstrated the destructiveness of the tongue and the words that roll off the tongue. If you look around today, it is no different. A loose mouth is the cause for so much of the world's damage in relationships, friendships, marriages, and even global conflicts.

The world consists of people who never learn to be silent. We are taught that we should not let anyone talk down to us or disrespect us, which is true, in a sense. Paul told Timothy in 1 Timothy in 4:12 Let no man despise thy youth; but be thou an example of the believers, in word, in conversation, in charity, in spirit, in faith, in purity, however this verse is Paul telling Timothy let your very actions as a believer be a voice to who you are. We are taught however the opposite in the world.

According to scripture, we are to let our righteousness do the speaking and not our mouth. God wants his people to stand up for an injustice because scripture tells us "justice" and only justice shall ye follow, but it also tells us "vengeance is mine saith the Lord." We are taught that if any man disrespects us verbally to tell him off because he is making you look less than a man/woman should look. What has to be realized is that in today's age and society, if I may be so blunt, people are insane nowadays. Since sin has increased in the world, so has the effect and fruits of sin increased. People's temper levels, and the occurrence of violent situations, mostly domestic and especially public, whether it be between a wife or a friend. One wrong word can tick a person off nowadays and the next thing you know, you are six feet below in a cardboard box. So because of sin and intolerance and low self-esteem, teachers are teaching, "don't let anybody walk over you or talk down to you," and "stand up for yourself," is breaking up more relationships, causing more job losses, and increasing more murder rates because people have not learned to work things out peacefully. However is it all the other person's fault or is it also ours?

Initially, this scripture is meant for the person who is doing the talking. It is meant for the person who thinks he/she can say whatever he/she wants without any repercussions. Scripture tells us that life and death are in the power of the tongue.

Scripture tells us in 1 Peter 2:17 to "Honour all men. Love the brotherhood." On the street, there is a level of respect that must be given to each man/woman. If you cross that line, you can say goodbye to this world. Many people wonder why so many of our young people get murdered on the street day in and day out. As said, it is sin of course, but the expression of that sin is a loose mouth. If a certain individual has a loose mouth and says something to an individual in the spirit that the Bible instructs us not to tell that person in love, then that person will take it as an insult and feel like he has been disrespected. Since he/she feels like he/she has been disrespected, he/she will take appropriate action to gain his/her respect back, usually with a .357 magnum. When a murder happens we usually look at the person doing the shooting and his temper instead of looking at what was SAID to him to make him react this way. As said, people can be enraged to murder for irrational reasons, a kind word being said, a pat on the shoulder, a glance or even a smile can cause someone to act in irrational ways. However, it can quickly and surely be triggered by an unkind word or gesture. Not only does the act have to be checked, but what caused the act to happen has to be analyzed also.

The reality of this scripture and the issue of the scripture is one of control and temperance.

Control of self and control of actions on both party sides. Because until an individual realizes that his/her words contain life and can bring life of an action into being, then as scripture tells us, he/she will always meet up with destruction.

WISDOM for the block:

When one talks without even thinking or consideration, that person has just signed his/her own contract for destruction.

Prayer – Father, I pray that my words will keep my life and not bring in my own death. Open my
mouth to speak your words and your thoughts, to
bring peace and not war between me and my brethren and sisters.

In Jesus Christ name, I pray.

Amen.

Lesson 4:

The soul of the sluggard desireth, and hath nothing, but the soul of the diligent shall be made fat.

(Proverbs 13:4)

I remember hearing a conversation somewhere where there were two guys talking. One said, "If I had a million dollars I would do absolutely nothing." The other man responded, "You don't need a million dollars to do that. Look at my cousin Clifford, he does nothing and sits on his behind every day!"

While the story is amusing, as the saying goes, it would be funny if it weren't true. It's amazing how we want things, which basically is our problem. Starting off we just want things. However, the things that we want, we are not willing to work to achieve them. We, of course, are silver spoon people, mostly in this society. We want things without working for it. If we are broke it's because we spend on material items, then we are broke because of the fact we never try to stay paid or learn the virtue of saving.

I heard one entertainer say once in a song, "I'm never down to my last dollar, I'm working first."[1] But we are just the opposite. We think that everything is going to come to us if we pray hard enough and wait on the Lord. True prayer and waiting are the keys to prosperity because you are putting your fate in the hands of Almighty God, but opportunities must be searched out.

Opportunities, unless they are out of your own will, do not fall into your lap. You must work for them and search them out. It's called "fish and bait mindset." If you want to catch fish, you have to put out your bait and wait. However, if you want to catch a number of fish, you must bait and put out many fishing poles. One of them will snag. If you don't have any bait or fishing poles, then how can you catch any fish?

People who lack work ethic are not only a nuisance in areas of money but in relationships, study, and anything that takes effort. Relationships take an effort to maintain because there will be rocky roads ahead in relationships. To battle through it and try with God's help to repair the damage done in the relationship takes work. Our schools are becoming a blackboard jungle. The first sign of a coming dictatorship is that of the failure of the education system. Once a person stops learning then he/she will be taught by someone else, because they are too lazy to critically analyze what they are hearing. I love atheists and anyone who is against the Word of God because the questions that are posed by these groups challenge me on my knowledge of the Word of God. Effort is taken if you are going to win an argument which there should not be between believers and non-believers alike, but scripture tells us to give an answer to every man who asks the reason for the hope that is within you. Study to show thyself approved; a workman needeth not be ashamed.

This is the spirit of the diligent. This is the spirit of the worker and this is the spirit of the one who will stay paid in any situation.

In the street, there is a saying, C.R.E.A.M. which stands for Cash Rules Everything Around Me. While we in Christ totally know that as a falsehood and God is the Maker, the owner and the designer of every situation and heart, lazy people or people without a plan are not respected on street level. So, as said, the point is not to strive to get rich but having a plan and working in that God-inspired plan to stay paid and more importantly working that talent or gift for the glory of God.

If you don't have a plan for what God wants you to do, just pray that God will give you an answer to what he wants you to do for Him and He will show you. When God assigns a person a project, it will not only bring that person to a closer relationship with Christ and manifest His glory, but it will bear fruit in your life, which provides not only for your spirit, but for your whole well-being.

WISDOM for the block:

If you don't want to be a sluggard don't live the life of a slug. Stay focused and busy for what God has given you to work with and you will be without want.

Prayer – Father, let us stick to the business of using the talents you have given us not only for material gain but also for building a better future and life for us and those in our community as we are constantly on our grind for you.

In Jesus Christ name, I pray.

Amen.

Lesson 5:

A righteous man hateth lying: but a wicked man is loathsome, and cometh to shame.

(Proverbs 13:5)

Is it safe to say that we have become a dishonest nation? Lies in the home, lies in the church, lies in the media, and even lies about and in government. We have become a nation of professional hypocrites. Why do we lie so much? What is there to achieve by lying and not being honest? Why is falsehood such a revered trait?

Knowing something about lying in my past life, I can give you some reasons why people lie. Two of the most well-known reasons are that it saves embarrassment of that person saying, "I told you so" or being judged and criticized harshly because they didn't tell the truth in the first place, and second we don't want to hurt another person's feelings. That is on a person-to-person level.

Something we will tackle right now then going on to the other reasons for lying and falsehood.

On a person-to-person level, when something needs to be told to another person and you know it will hurt that person's feelings, of course it is natural to feel sympathy for that person; we don't want to hurt that person's feelings because he/she is so close to us that we can't bear hurting them. In our own wisdom, we don't tell them news that might hurt them or make up a story not to stress that person out. The reality is that God is in control of every heart and is the one who decides who lives or dies. He is the controller of all and is in all. God works through reality and truth and manifests himself through reality and truth, to bring people to a realization about a situation. By lying about a certain situation, we keep God from helping that person rectify the situation if possible before it gets out of hand. Lying cannot accomplish this because lying is with self and not the needs of others. It is meant to save face basically, which brings us to our next reason for lying, embarrassment.

Then there are other reasons for lying. Whether it be lies to spouses, friends, or even in the corporate arena. These lies are meant to save face; and if we keep the lie long enough we can fix this situation and once this situation is repaired we can really just tell the truth and they will understand and everything will be hunky dory. The situation may be fixed but it was done while sitting on dishonesty while doing it.

Scripture tells us that a righteous man hateth lying simply because lying is of the devil. As said, I can testify to that as dishonesty was in my heart as well, and the scripture compares a lying man to a wicked man who is loathsome and cometh to shame. Ever think how liars end up? They are blasted on newspapers and tabloids for cheating on their wives, or cheating on their taxes, or even cheating on their friends, all of which is composed of a lie. Satan's method to get Eve to eat the apple was deception. From that point on, the world as you see it by media, books, and entertainers is just walking, talking, lies, trying to sell you what the devil wants you to have and not what God intended you to have.

Another thing is God's character and His detestment of lying. One thing about lying that brought me to my knees is the fact of God's character of truth and how He hates liars. Scripture tells us in Psalm 101:7, He that worketh deceit shall not dwell within my house: he that telleth lies shall not tarry in my sight.

This brought me to my knees and still brings me to my knees in repentance. To know that liars will not tarry in God's sight and also there is a promise in Revelations 21:8 that liars will have their part in the lake of fire. That really shook me to my knees.

God is all truth and there is no lie in Him. To come to Christ is to come to truth and see the reality of a situation. Jesus said in the last day, ALL shall be revealed, there will be no cover up.

Wouldn't you like to live a life of no cover ups instead of ducking under the cloak of a lie all the time? Trust me after a while this just gets really old really fast.

In life, we will all mess up. We will all make mistakes and we all foul up. While we strive for perfection in
Christ Jesus, we have to realize we are incomplete creatures and will only be made truly complete when we are in heaven. But out of this, we concern ourselves so

much with the fact that we messed up; that we don't fess up to the crime. A mistake in our eyes makes us look less of a man or a woman and puts a doubt in our mind (obviously from the devil) telling us *"I thought you could handle this...what are you going to do now?"* We cover our mistake up with a lie. It beats being called a loser or a chump right? Like I said, being an expert in lying in the past, I do know some things. However, a true man fesses up to his mistakes. It shows character to say, Yeah, I messed up and I am sorry; more importantly, it says to the devil, "Yeah, I messed up…AND? I may fall but I will get up. I will start again." The devil will plant in your mind that it's over, just save yourself the embarrassment and tell them what *didn't* happen to save face. God is never like that and strengthens us by making us face the consequences.

Even though lying may seem convenient for the moment and save face, trust me, the consequences it brings as far as being viewed as an untrustworthy person are far worse. Even though I know it's easier to tell a lie rather than to tell a truth and look like an idiot for what you did however, in the long run people will know you as
an honorable man/woman; as one who tells the truth and also one who is human and does make mistakes and fesses up to them.

WISDOM for the block:

We all have a tendency to be liars, but as far as being a nation of liars, where are the real people who are of truth? Just be a real person and strive to be honest in all your dealings.

Prayer – Lord, you are the author of all truth. Not just some but all. May we all imitate your spirit and may truth pass through our minds and our
spirits so that we can start being real people that can be trusted and not bring shame through our dishonesty.

In Jesus Christ name, I pray.

Amen.

Lesson 6:

Righteousness keepeth him that is upright in the way: but wickedness overthroweth the sinner.

(Proverbs 13:6)

If you are a boxer or have ever boxed there is one word that is crucial to winning any match that you are engaged in. This little word is called focus, the one crucial trait that can majorly decide whether the match will go in your favor or not, especially if you let emotions get in your way. If you let anger get in the way while you are in a boxing match, then your focus will be shifted and you will lose the match.

This is the same way that unrighteous behavior throws us and takes us down. It keeps us from doing right and sends us down a path that is constantly destructive. Concerns with image, issues of life, emotions, and even little trite issues can pull us directly from the way of God and down the devil's path of destruction. Righteousness keeps your mind clear to make and see the right decisions you have to make that are in front of you and not to decisions that might lead to a risk to your life and well-being.

John chapter 10:10 tells us that the devil came to steal, kill, and destroy. Steal what? Your car, your jewels, your possessions? The devil is not concerned about that. Maybe we are but the devil isn't. The thing that the devil wants to steal is your peace of mind, which is usually connected to your cars, jewels, money, and your women.

What does he come to kill? Your life? The devil can lead you down a road where you do just that but in the devil's case, he wants to kill everything in your life that is leading to the path of God. Remember he is a murderer. He just doesn't do it physically or at least cause it to happen physically, he does it in a way that is more damaging. He does it psychologically through the mind. Because once he can kill or capture a thought then he knows that the rest is simple where we destroy ourselves. Instead of resting in Christ, we rest in the liquor bottle. Instead of putting our cares in the Lord, we put our cares into what people think of us. This is the murderous mindset of the devil. What does he destroy? Anything that brings up a root in Christ Jesus. This is his mission and goal in life, to destroy any fruit that God brings or sprouts up in us because as Jesus said in John 15:1 that he was "the true vine." It is Satan's job to cut us off from that vine.

However scripture does not stop there, in John 15:10, Jesus says I am come that they might have life, and that they might have it more abundantly; meaning that Jesus came that we will have a life that leads us down a road of life and not death. He keeps our focus and keeps us from being overthrown. Every time Satan is mentioned in scripture, death is not too far behind.

St. Paul said in 1 Corinthians 9:26: "I therefore so run, not as uncertainly; so fight I, not as one that beateth the air." In other words, He has control and focus, focus as to look ahead when I run and focus even when I fight, so that every hit I land will connect. Focus is the central trait not only to being a boxer but also central to being a man of God. Let us keep our minds and hearts focused on what God has and tells us and not let Satan overthrow us with his devices off the right path.

WISDOM for the block:

Can a car make you right? Can the right girl/guy make you right? Can having money in your pocket make you right? The only thing that will make you right and not stumble in life, is a relationship with Christ Jesus and submission to God alone because God is the author of everything that is right and everything that will cause you not to get caught up by the devil, in the streets and in this life.

Prayer - We thank you God for being the source of all that is right, all that is straight and all that is pure. I thank you Jesus today for putting us on a straight path and continue to put us on a straight path so that we will not be caught up in this world but walk a straight path for you.

In Jesus Christ name, I pray.

Amen.

Lesson 7:

There is that maketh himself rich, yet hath nothing: there is that maketh himself poor, yet hath great riches.

(Proverbs 13:7)

When Muhammad Ali went over to the country of Zaire in the famous Rumble in the Jungle match against George Foreman, one of the things he told the African people of Zaire was "You are so much better than us." He continued by saying, "Yes, in America we may have more money and power, but you are able to show something in your poverty that we just don't have in America, the power of dignity." Muhammad Ali stated something that many people who look at third world constantly miss through their view of third world countries. That is that money, power, and wealth cannot and does not make you happy or cause happiness within a person. If you observe third world countries such as Africa you may see extreme poverty but you will see the greatest examples of brotherhood and dignity and non-compromising behavior that America could not duplicate in a million years. We focus on how poor these people are because we believe that money makes or adds on to a person's happiness and provides for all their needs. Now money does provide for a person's needs, but not all. Almost every time when money is given to a certain locale, fights and wars are not too far behind.

Our usual view in America is to look at people as unfortunate because they have no money, instead of looking at what that person has that money cannot buy. It is said in Thailand where Muay Thai kick boxing was originated, kick boxers make themselves poor because they believe that the more poor they are the more hungry they will be in their training. Not because they want a certain amount of fame after they win a certain amount of matches, but it is because they believe that money and power will be a distraction to their training and focus.

This scripture tells us There is that maketh himself rich, yet hath nothing: there is that maketh himself poor, yet hath great riches. Think about that. Every day the mantra is said, "If I had a million dollars I would be set for life!" If we take a look at the wealthy and the influential we will see just the opposite. There are more divorces in families with money than there are in families without money. The people who just inherited money because of luck or chance will tell you that they wish they never had the money in the first place. Rarely, you hear someone say, "Getting this million dollars has really changed my life for the better!" Many people however, do make this statement but it is only because they said they did not see what they had even before them money came. It is replaced with an attitude of pride and ego because of the realization of they were here and they acted with a humble attitude only because they didn't have the money but now that they are rich they can act any way they want to. We say that money doesn't change a person, but it just shows the person that you truly are because now you can afford to be the person you TRULY are now. The nothingness that scripture talks about money not buying is the attitude that we have towards others once the money comes and how pride and ego manifest into a person once money now becomes part of their lives. Paul tells Timothy in 1 Timothy 6:17: "Charge them that are rich in this world, that they be not high-minded, nor trust in uncertain riches, but in the living God, who giveth us richly all things to enjoy." Turn on any music station or entertainment show and you are sure to see some rapper or so called celebrity boasting about how he or she was poor and now because they are successful they are in a better place now because they are rich. The reason they are acting in a different way and manner because he didn't have anything before. As said, it seems when money is acquired, humility and dignity are also lost and what is given in its place are pride and unrighteousness in its place. It is no sin to be rich, but as Paul said to Timothy. It is a sin to think that because you are rich that you have power. Remember, the one who made the earth is the same one who made the sun which gives nourishment to the grass, which grows the tree, which is chopped down to make the money. (Whew! You see how long the process is?) Without Him, you would have no money to boast about. The true riches that God talks about us already possessing and that money can never possess, is that of his Word and the joy and true peace of mind that it brings. In all things let us, as scripture says, strive not for that which is incorruptible or as Jesus said, men will break through and steal. Even as testified once by Hip Hop Emcee and Producer Dr. Dre, money will buy a lot of things, but is peace of mind one of them?

WISDOM for the block:

Jesus told us in Matthew 13:44: "Again, the kingdom of heaven is like unto treasure hid in a field; the which when a man hath found, he hideth, and for joy thereof goeth and selleth all that he hath, and buyeth that field."

When you are righteous, nothing in this world is worth living in a life that is right. No jewels, or money in the world can compare to living a good life unto God, worthy of His respect. Everything you own will fade away, but the walk of a righteous man is eternal.

Prayer – Father, scripture says that your Word is a precious jewel. Let me cherish and see the richness of your Word over the riches of this world and the things the world tries to promote as riches.

In Jesus Christ name, I pray.

Amen.

Lesson 8:

The ransom of a man's life are his riches: but the poor heareth not rebuke.

(Proverbs 13:8)

"Gimme $10,000 in unmarked bills or you will never see little Timmy alive again!" Have you ever heard such words when looking at a movie about a kidnapping? As we know, this phenomenon is not only taking place in the movies we watch, but in the world today as a growing epidemic. Teenage girls and boys in America are being kidnapped and held hostage for some strange reason or another, with a demand that a certain amount of money be given for their release. Overseas it's the same scenario where Americans are held by military coups and their captors demand a certain political action to take place. Not to mention the trade of human trafficking which is kidnapping young ladies against their will to work for a John who forces them to work as a prostitute under the threat of harm to themselves or their families. I would like to stop now and tell the abortionist as I'm reading these incidents, if you still think that human life is still not precious, you are dead wrong!

Human life is one of the most precious elements that God has given to this planet. It is one of his greatest creations and should be given the greatest care and maturation on a physical, emotional, and spiritual level as Paul tells us in 1 Thessalonians 5:23. Our scripture is asking a very unique and if you look at it in a certain way, funny question. Why is it that men are kidnapped for cash?

Is money *that important* to a person to turn a family's life upside down in a matter of hours or minutes? Not playing devil's advocate, but a look from the inside view of things clearly shows it's not all about the money, it's about giving up something that means utterly nothing for a life that could not equal all the money in the world. That is how precious life is, an expendable item for an indispensable life. Money even has a value over human life and will be traded in exchange for a human life. The more money a person has, the more he/she is a target to be kidnapped because of his/her money. You know how it is said, more money, more problems. Try telling that however, to the person who has no money.

This cannot only be seen in human life exchanges
but also in business and life in general. On street level, a certain amount of crack cocaine can be exchanged for a certain amount of money. On the business side, money is exchanged for a certain area of viable land. Prostitutes and night club dancers exploit and sell their very bodies for dollars to pay their rent or for the quick dough. The reason for this is because money has been given a value over human life and especially human dignity and character. It was the rapper Jadakiss that said once in a

verse, "Ain't no way I'm gonna let this money get past me, when all I had to do in the first place was to get nasty." We will gladly exchange human dignity for money because we see no real value in it. We say to ourselves what is the worth of human dignity and character? It's not paying my rent! It's not getting me out of this hole that I am in! We are glad to trade human dignity and respect for money. As scripture tells us, the ransom of a man's life is his riches. That is what it takes away, his very life, the life that God intended us to have; the image that God intended us to have.

We would trade it in a minute for a quick dollar, knowing that scripture tells us that God will provide all our needs according to Philippians 4:19. We don't have to exchange the corruptible for the incorruptible to pay our rent or to get the things we need. God will supply all our needs and will never have us begging bread as David once said. Trust is a key factor here, not trusting in things that will perish or are corruptible, but in the things that will last past money. Like the Word of God and the things that He instructs us to do. That will last even past this whole world; trust on that.

I said there was a humorous part about this. The question was asked why are men kidnapped for cash, but the second part of this question should be why are poor men not subject to that? Well, it's in the question basically. Because they are poor! Have you ever seen a rap emcee who has a lot of riches never carry a bodyguard or a gun around with him? It is because his riches has put him in a place where his very life is sometimes in jeopardy from people who want to see him go down. The poor don't have to deal with such toils. With all due respect, what is it that a robber could take as a ransom from the poor? Nothing really, because even their dwellings alone tell them that this person has nothing they can use, so they will go to another person's house who has more. That in itself is a true blessing, not to be worried if someone is going to rob your house or your possessions. Not to say it won't happen but you can be rest assured that it is very rarely in your situation that it does. The poor from a closer view has a most definite advantage over the rich in many situations and cases. The question is, what is the ransom on a man's life? The thing that the world puts a value on, which is something that is more valuable to that person than human life itself. The question that must be asked, is a certain thing important over the God who created it?

The second part of why the poor does not hear rebuke is because not only because they are poor is because of their actions they are put into poverty. Ask how many millionaires have spent, and spent, and spent, and spent some more and now they are truly broke because they didn't listen to sound advice. Money is not object was their motto and life creed so they spent without any sound advice on how to use that money.

The Bible tells us in Proverbs 4:7 "Wisdom is the principal thing; therefore get wisdom: and with all thy getting get understanding." What is wisdom worth?

According to Proverbs 8:11 "wisdom is better than rubies; and all the things that may be desired are not to be compared to it." Nothing.

We become broke because we chase after things that make us broke ultimately, but if we chase after God's wisdom we become more wise because we have something that this world can not put a price tag on and that's God's knowledge and wisdom that the world cannot take and the world cannot steal because wisdom on how to deal with a certain situation, wisdom on how to deal with a certain problem, wisdom on how to make the right decision is better than having a million dollars in your hand which cannot advise you, which cannot tell you the right way to go, and certainly not give you peace because even that goes away, so as the scripture says Get wisdom and Get understanding.

Stop being broke all your life but focus on getting that which is better than all the money in the world and that's God's wisdom and the peace that goes with it.

WISDOM for the block:

Christ paid the price for us. Nothing can compare to our lives because our lives are precious to us and God. The next time you drink an alcoholic beverage, smoke a little weed, or hold a gun up to someone and about to take their life, remember that all our lives were bought with a price.

Prayer - Please Lord, let us know over everything else your Word is worth and over all the riches that men can produce in this world.

In Jesus Christ name, we pray.

Amen.

Lesson 9:

The light of the righteous rejoiceth: but the lamp of the wicked shall be put out.

(Proverbs 13:9)

You know how you hear the old saying, "Here today, gone tomorrow?" That is the path that the man/woman who does not follow God and his precepts follow when they decide to go their own way. Men in some way shape, form or fashion still think they are bulletproof and can do anything they please with no consequence attached to it. This is just plain foolishness and stupidity. Everything, whether good, bad or otherwise, has a consequence to it. Sir Isaac Newton called it the Law of Opposites, where for every action there is an equal and opposite reaction, or another way to put it is the Law of Cause and Effect where simply put for every cause there is an effect.

This proverb tells us that the light of the righteous rejoiceth: but the lamp of the wicked shall be put out. Why do the righteous rejoiceth? Because he is doing the right thing and making the right decisions based on God's Word, and not to be arrogant, but another reason that he rejoiceth is because he is looking at how the world around him is going down in some way or another and he/she is still standing. Scripture tells us in Psalms 1:3 And he shall be like a tree planted by the rivers of water, that bringeth forth his fruit in his season; his leaf also shall not wither; and whatsoever he doeth shall prosper. However, is this attitude practiced today? Of course not! Why? Mainly because it contests itself against everything that the world teaches. Also, it cuts into areas that we are not ready to relinquish yet unto God; areas like reputation. Keep this one fact in mind, Jesus said one of the fruits of doing right is that you will get ridiculed. You will get ostracized; you will get called a chump; you will get called a geek; you will get called a nerd; you will be called a square. You will get called on not keeping it real. The question that must be asked is what is reputation and what is it worth? Reputation may gain you respect with your family members, friends, co-workers and even your crew, but it also takes something away from you in exchange for that, like deciding to truly make a right decision. When you deal with reputation, you only deal with what is good to keep a reputation and an image and not what is good for what is common sense and especially reality.

Reputation will tell you that you are not a man/woman if you haven't engaged in some form of sexual activity. Reputation will tell you if you let people punk and make you look like a sissy then you are a chump. Reputation says if you are more interested in science and deeper things of thought then you are a geek or a nerd. Reputation will tell you if you are not wearing the hottest outfit on then you are not keeping it real or not even one to relate to. Reputation may bring you these things, but what reputation does not tell you is the result of these things. Remember what I said, reputation takes away a certain something from you. You may be not be viewed as a man or a woman by society for not having sex, but pass by the local clinic and see how many people who thought they were men or women by thinking that having sex was the thing to do. You may be viewed as a chump for not defending yourself and letting everything slide. But Jesus just didn't say in Matthew chapter 5:10 "Blessed are they which are persecuted for righteousness' sake: for theirs is the kingdom of heaven" just to waste breath. He was saying it for a reason. Jesus brought peace, a peace as St. Paul says in Philippians 4:7 "which passeth all understanding, shall keep your hearts and minds through Christ Jesus." The sinner has to CARE about reputation, CARE about being called a chump, but the purpose of God's Word is to put all your CARES on him. This new attitude gives you headway not to care about man's foolish laws and to even bring up the question, Okay, why am I following this again for some other persons respect? And what about wearing the hottest gear? Jesus told us that all these things will pass away. Fashion changes with the wink of an eye. You ever heard the term slave to fashion? That's what most people are nowadays. Because they follow what's hot and what's in without really having intelligence to question why it is hot and in. The dress of women today are now looking more like the dresses of night walkers, and men's dress are looking more like the dress of a Hip Hop court jester or a celebrity playboy. We do this to be recognized by this society. The question is, Why?

This is why the righteous man rejoiceth because he is not bound by this world's rules. He is the true one who can truly say he is not bound by rules or what society dictates to him/her. The sinner, as scripture continues and says that the lamp of the wicked shall be put out. Is it that serious? Trust me, if you follow the ways of man, you will physically or spiritually go down; especially as this scripture is pushing a definition of the physical; if you go back to the reputation example on not defending yourself. How many people do you know tried to defend their honor and now they are six feet deep for doing so? God main purpose in His Word is to tell us not to get entangled into man's arguments or his doings, or basically don't come down to his beastly level of thought, because as scripture tells us, his lamp shall be put out, meaning that one way or another whether spiritually, mentally, or physically, the unrighteous will go down. The wages of sin is death and following that road will only find you laying on an outline of chalk on the sidewalk made by the police department in a homicide because you had to defend that you called your manhood. It's just that real.

The question that has to be asked here is what road will I follow? The way of life or the way of death? It may not be as popular, but life is not a popularity contest, life is real, and God is the realest thing on this planet earth and in the galaxy. He is the dominant factor overall and supersedes man's thoughts and actions and guides us on the right path to life that will not have us on a road to tears or death, but on a road to rejoicing as scripture tells us, because we know that we have followed the ways of the Word, and found the ways of men to be utter foolishness. Let us not have our lamps put out but rather let's rejoice because we are free from the world's oppressive rules and behavior that the world puts on us, and truly follow Christ Jesus our Lord. Amen.

WISDOM for the block:

Reputation may mean something in this world to different persons, but nothing to the one who created the world and is no respecter of persons.

Prayer – Lord let me follow the ways of your Word which is right and true, and do not let me fall into the trap of following the world and its ways of death and its methods of gaining respect. God you are the lifter up of all men so in you will I trust.

In Jesus Christ name I pray

Amen.

Lesson 10:

Only by pride cometh contention: but with the well advised is wisdom.

(Proverbs 13:10)

Why do friendships end? Why do relationships bend? Why do marriages falter even before they hit the altar? We can give a lot of reasons but there is one seed that stems from all of it and that is the seed of pride. Almost every evil and contentious thought and action comes from the fruit of pride. In this society, it is a sin to let a person run all over you or not get your proper respect. This attitude has been the attitude that has broken up more marriages, more friendships, and more relationships because pride planted a seed telling us, "I know you are not going to let him talk to you like that!" To try to resolve the conflict in a peaceful manner would be ludicrous because that is a violation of our own respect and people want to see you stand up for yourself right? Or is it just pride that wants to see you stand up for yourself?

Pride always tells us to get our respect and get what's coming to us. Pride tells us that someone embarrassed us and it is our job to get respect or end the relationship quickly. Pride is always telling us not to let anyone walk over you.

In the end pride wins the battle as we are left without a friendship or relationship because of it. "I wish he/she could hear my side of it.", "I wish they could understand how I felt." "I wish I could explain to them of how this is hurting me!" One of the most dangerous letters in the Christian language always seems to be the main letter that we hold onto dearly; that letter is the letter "I". I'm entitled; I'm worthy; I'm right! Pride always causes contention because it will always block that person off from seeing one half of the truth.

David asks in Psalms 8:4, what is mankind, that thou art mindful of him? And the son of man, that thou visitest him? He asks firstly, what is man? Better yet, what has to be asked is, who is man? What privileges and authority does he have or should he have? Should he have any at all? Who is he? The Word says that our righteousness is as filthy as rags. Everything we do is filthy. There is none that doeth good, no, not one. Psalms 14:3. All of our man made inventions that we have created without the guidance of God in this world has only led to more wars, more fights, more battles, and more breakups. The only one that is able to hold things together is the one who has Godly wisdom. Godly wisdom brings peace to a situation and light to a dark space. It looks within a situation and fixes the gap that is missing from the issue. Over a million dollars a year is spent on therapists who try to fix what the Word of God can fix in ten seconds.

Wisdom shows you how to survive on street level because pride is the main thing that usually gets a person murdered. Pride of shoes, pride of outfit, pride of thinking that you are the man/woman when as the rapper Nas put it, "You are smaller than an Ashanti tribe in an African village."[1] Pride is the motivating fuel for most breakups in circles and crews. Wisdom advises a person in the right direction or tries to bridge the gap that is missing in an issue between two people without it getting to a boil and something happening that you wished never happened. It calms the situation down to a simmer regardless of losing face in front of your crew. Because God is no respecter of persons and he expects the same out of his believers. To be a respecter of no man ultimately except God, or in other words, image is not important when a relationship and heart could be repaired.

Pride causes great contention between two parties; it is the main gate between two individuals, but Jesus came to break that gate and to make that gate disappear. Jesus at the beginning of Matthew chapter 5 gives us outlining principles for breaking contention. But one of the main tenants of that sermon is when he said, "Blessed are the peacemakers: for they shall be called the children of God." This is our goal to be peacemakers and not breakers; to squash beef, conflict, and pride. When Jesus was crucified on the cross, He crucified not only himself, but I was nailed on the cross with him. It is our duty to nail ourselves to the cross and let it die there and live

---

[1] "No Ideas Original" Nas, The Lost Tapes, 2002

fruitfully in His law so that pride will not have any more root in our lives; especially the lives of others that are in our life whether it be crew or family. Pride brings contention, but wisdom brings the answer of peace in a situation. Seek wisdom and you will find peace.

WISDOM for the block:

Pride creates a box where you are trapped by your own greatness. Wisdom shows that there is something greater than you. Know that no man is an island. There is someone that created everything that you see and only He is worthy of boasting about and lifting up, and not ourselves or anything we have done.

Prayer - O Lord, let us seek peace in every situation and state. Satan brings pride but you bring the answer. Give us wisdom to retain peace and not pride.

In Jesus Christ name, we pray

Amen.

Lesson 11:

Wealth gotten by vanity shall be diminished, but he that gathereth by labour shall increase.

(Proverbs 13:11)

"Vanity! Vanity! All is vanity!!" So quipped the writer of Ecclesiastes. Right now it can probably be translated in "Bling! Bling! All is Bling!" Or "Money, Money, Money, All is Money!" It is impossible to turn on the television without a celebrity whether in the movie or music business (mostly music) talking about his/her wealth and how being hooked up or connected with a certain record label or industry provided the way for them to amass such wealth. Wealth itself is not gained totally from being affiliated with this or that talent agent or music mogul, but it is gained from what that actor or artist produces and the number of people that swarm to buy it.

As one new artist put it Leela James asks in her song, Music, she wonders "Where did the music go, and why don't we sing no more."

Actress Halle Berry was paid an estimated $500,000 for a full frontal nude scene in the movie Swordfish, and became the first African American woman ever to win an

Oscar for her sex scene in Monster's Ball. Rapper Lloyd Banks stated himself in the song Fire "These dudes are getting the wrong deals. I'm 21 sittin on mills." Stating a reality that it is possible in this day and age, to be only just 21 years old and now get a million dollar record deal. Money is gained off of what people are feeding off of at the time and right now what people are being fed and force fed day in and day out right now is the feast of violence, vanity, and of course, extreme sexual content. In Hip Hop and urban culture now, the ideology has denigrated into seeing no way out of the situation, so the only way to get money is to hustle and sell drugs or do some other illegal activity, be good at some type of sport or get a contract with the NFL or the NBA, or even the NBL; or have nice rap skills and get a record deal. This is the trapped mentality of the hood and the community now. This is the mentality that is also talked about in the records.

However, the question that the proverb is asking us is why is our main sources of income gained off of everything that seeks to destroy ourselves and our dignity and character and also will not last? As scripture tells us What profiteth a man that he gained the whole world and lose his soul? His soul is usually referring to his natural being that makes that person an original. We did not all come in this world wanting to be a superstar singer, or a superstar actor. Most of us had humble occupations in mind of being a doctor, a lawyer, or even a fireman.

Something to help the place where we had our first beginnings. Vanity gained off of marketing

and selling what the public wants, and what the public wants to hear and what the public wants to see us as only destroys the culture and community we are coming from. We love Paris Hilton's, the P'Diddy's, The Warren Buffets, The Kardashians, but what is it that they are selling that we love them so much?

As said, the public only feeds and buys what is the popular philosophy of the time. Since it tends to be sexuality and not sensibility, and rebellion and not righteousness, then this is what the public will buy. We have become consumers of vanity and violence, sex and sensuality. We destroy ourselves in the process and don't mature as many artists would have you to think, so we pay gladly for the destruction of ourselves.

The other half of this proverb gives a solution to this situation. Do labor; honest, dignified labor. Labor that brings not only monetary gain out of it but also strengthens and encourages the character and dignity one has, not only of oneself but the community to which one belongs. The thing about most of the sexual movies and violence that come out nowadays is that, it's so simple to do. Anybody, I mean anybody can go in a studio think of some foul lyrics and then they have a hit record. All that is needed is to hide it under a nice beat or some type of innuendo "Wait till you see my..." and you got a smash record. I think it was one rap emcee that said in a rhyme once, "I got tired of my job, so I decided to do yours."

Money is gained off of something that takes little brain power to create. However, scripture says something and instructs something totally different. True labor gained by work that is honest and pure and brings godly values and virtues out of an individual is what God intends us to do. Charles Spurgeon, one of the greatest preachers in the world, once said, "Accept always the humblest occupation or position." I think it was Bill Gates that said something to the effect of, "Do not not consider flipping burgers beneath your dignity. In the old days, your parents had a different word for it. They called it opportunity."

The question is however, which one will last longer? Wealth gained by what the culture dictates is hot or in will only last a few years because it is what the culture dictates is hot at the time. There will always be a need for doctors, teachers, chemists, landscapers, architects, and computer scientists because these fields are always in need and evolving. I believe it was someone who stated once that knowledge is infinite, meaning knowledge only builds and evolves. Striving for things gained and promoting vanity will not stand.

The question that has to be asked is, even though you have gained the wealth and power, what did you lose in

return to gain that wealth and power? Remember that you cannot gain anything in life without losing something in return, usually something of equal and substantial value. One thing will take away from another. The wealth and love of this world will take away the wealth of character and take away the focus of the first love, which is God.

Our lesson for today teaches never put your trust in wealth that will be diminished in a few years' time and takes your soul and respect along with it. However put your effort into occupations that not only builds a sense of dignity and respect not only because it shows character inside and outside of you, but it also builds for others and encourages others to build.

WISDOM for the block:

We all see the glitz and glam of what the "stars" have but what about the true stars that make sure we are safe from harm; or make sure that people are saved from a fire; or the people that keep the roads paved so we can ride our Maybach Benz on them? While being a success in the public eye is great, the most meager of jobs demand the utmost respect because they support everything that everybody else does.

Prayer - Please God, place us in an occupation
that is not based on the vanity of this culture but on
the greatness that You have placed inside of us to build and create.

In Jesus Christ name, we pray

Amen.

Lesson 12:

Hope deferred maketh the heart sick, but when the desire cometh, it is a tree of life.

(Proverbs 13:12)

"What happens to a dream deferred? Does it dry up like a raisin in the sun? Or fester like a sore—
And then run?"[2]

Langston Hughes asked the question, what happens to a dream that is deferred? What happens when what you spent your whole life hoping on, working on, is just smashed right in your face? It seems that every door is shut right in your face! The word "No" seems to be on the lips of everybody that you ask for a chance. Everywhere there is an "I'm sorry" or "We have chosen someone else" or "We regret to inform you.." These rejections have the power to kill dreams and murder aspirations. The words "I'm sorry" says enough to kill a dream. Or can it? On street level when speaking about dreams, hopes and aspirations, thank God there is one

word that the true warrior of the street hasn't learned yet, and that word is "Quit." There is no such thing as quit in

---
[2] "Harlem" Langston Hughes, Harlem, 1951

the human language to the true warrior of the street, simply because too much is at stake. Rapper Fifty Cent said once about his career, "We came to the point when we started rapping that this has to work, there was no plan B."

What Fifty did was box himself in a corner where there was no option but to succeed, because there was no plan B. We hear the sermon all the time about how Jesus told the disciples to cast their nets on the other side of the boat and you will catch some fish, meaning maybe you ought to try a new way. Many people take that and leave the dream and destiny that God blessed them to follow other pursuits because maybe "This just wasn't in God's will for me to pursue." Abraham had to cross treacherous terrain to reach the promised land. Jesus said in Matthew 7:13-14: "Enter ye in at the strait gate: for wide is the gate, and broad is the way, that leadeth to destruction, and many there be which go in thereat: Because strait is the gate, and narrow is the way, which leadeth unto life, and few there be that find it." Strictly meaning that challenging man is God's way of bringing the fire and true character out of man. Something you got easy is not a victory unless you really prepared yourself for it; it is the challenge that really pulls something out of you that you have to look for. Beating some guys at basketball who really didn't have their A-game on in the first place is not a victory. It is beating opponents who have more

hunger than you do and will not let you win that will bring the true character out of you.

There is fortunately on street level never a dry spell of hope; simply because desire is always there. Like our scripture says desire is the tree of life. Our eyes are kept on the prize too much for us to quit and for our hope to be deferred. There is no deference of hope on the street. There is only the grind! This HAS GOT to work. This plan HAS GOT to work. There is no plan B. Maybe there are other choices but I'm moving toward what God has set my feet to do and what we want to achieve.

Before we end this lesson, I want to talk about the things you should desire to have. The American Dream and everything in it is a facade. It is a propaganda gimmick to lure you away from what God wants you to achieve. The first thing beyond anything is God wants you to love Him with your whole heart, whole soul, whole mind, whole strength and seek His face or seek His presence daily so that you can live like Him. Which means that the first desire is to be holy. Not to have cars, houses, beautiful women, or the Al Pacino "Scarface" fantasy world that the world seems to be casting their eyes on. Anything that does not shine God through it, will face destruction and is headed down the road of destruction. Do not strive to be the next hot entertainer or hot rapper, because trust me, maybe in the eyes of people this will last because it is kept alive by the people, but in God's eyes it is just vanity. Strive towards those things that build not only community but also a man's intellectual and spiritual character as well. More engineers are needed to build the next millennium far more than another entertainer who keeps us lazy watching the tube for hours on end.

Today's lesson teaches that man's "No" is actually God's "Yes." When our hopes are dashed against the rock, keep your eyes always on what you are striving for, depending what you are striving to get.

If your pursuits are noble and honorable in character and are meant to build up your community or shines the light of God through the pursuit, then do not quit. It is God's destiny for you to reach the promised land. It will be hard but hey, life isn't any picnic right?

WISDOM for the block:

Every time you hear "No" it should push you on to hear "Yes." When you hear "Don't" always hear that voice that says "Do." When every time you hear the word "Can't" switch your mind to "Yes, I can!" That is the mentality of the hustle and the one who is a success.

Prayer – Lord, please let us strive towards the noblest occupations and let the "No's" we receive in and from this world, be only your "Yes" to keep going for the prize.

In Jesus Christ name, we pray.

Amen.

Lesson 13

Whoso despiseth the Word shall be destroyed, but he that feareth the commandment shall be rewarded.

(Proverbs 13:13)

Why are there so many shootings going on? Why is there so much violence going on? Why is there chronic unemployment? Why is there so much civil unrest? This is the question of the hour that has been asked in many ways. Why? This is not a Jadakiss video although the answer to all his questions to why there is so much violence and hatred in the world today can be summed up in one word and that is…The Word!

The Word of God is why everything is going wrong in the world today, but please don't misunderstand. It is not the Word that is causing the problem, but the lack of obedience to it is why the world is becoming more like Satan's playground and not God's paradise that He originally intended it to be.

This scripture tells us those whoso despiseth the Word shall be destroyed. You may say I am not obeying the Word and I am not dead yet. Maybe not physically, but what about your spirit, finances, your relationships, your community, how's that been? Are there still shootings in your community and violence still in your home? It is a lack of following God's Word and His precepts.

VH-1 once did a summary of 40 of the most awful songs. Bette Midler's "From a distance" gained recognition as an awful song because of the main message that "God is watching us" implying that God is just sitting up there watching us and not doing anything while all types of evil happens to us. I believe scripture has an answer to why God is not moving to help us.

First, according to Proverbs 3:5, he is telling us that we are leaning on our own understanding; meaning we want to get our own gain and get what we want the way WE want to get it, instead of asking council from God or following God's plan about how to get it. God first cannot move to help us one inch because we are still doing things in our own power instead of moving in the power, instead of consulting with God and following His Word about the matter.

Second, according to Proverbs 3:7, we are wise in our own eyes. We already know how to get the dollars; we know what to do to get the money; we know what to do and how to survive. Scripture tells us to not to be wise in our own eyes and not pray for wisdom like James 1:5 "If any of you lack wisdom, let him ask of God, that giveth to all men liberally, and upbraideth not; and it shall be given him." First, our problem, once again comes from not asking God about the situation and asking for His guidance. James 4:1-2 tells us, "From whence come wars and fightings among you? come they not hence, even of your lusts that war in your members? Ye lust, and have not: ye kill, and desire to have, and cannot obtain: ye fight and war, yet ye have not, because ye ask not." Many people want but they don't ask God. The things sometimes that they want are not within God's will and plan for their lives, so they don't get it. Analyze about the things that you desire and why you want them.

There is a solution. Scripture tells us there is a way to be rewarded with what God wants us to have according to His will and purpose, and that is to fear His commandments; meaning to follow and not cross the commandments and things that God tells you to do. Once you do that, then everything from beginning to end will start to change. God is righteousness exemplified; He is the living essence of righteousness. To follow God is to follow all that is right. Following God means forsaking our plans and methods and following His way because our plans are useless and produce useless things.

You will see your community and life change as you become more disciplined, able to focus more on what is real from that which is false or fake because righteousness and the things of righteousness have taken hold and root. Scripture says in 2 Chronicles 7:14: "If my people which are called by my name, shall humble themselves, and pray, seek my face, and turn from their wicked ways; then I will hear from heaven, and will forgive their sin, and heal their land." That's all there is to do. Pray, spend time with God day in and day out, study and meditate on His Word. Let the Word minister and master your spirit and take you from the foolish things of this world, and He will heal your land of all corruption and evil. Turning to the Word, is the only way to restore everything back to God's goodness and to turn to God and His Word.

Today's lesson teaches if you want your life, home, community to be on everything it can be, you have to master yourself and let Christ be your master and follow the Word of God, because everything else if you didn't notice already is simply destruction of self.

WISDOM for the block:

We can follow the word on the street or the Word of God. The question is, which will lead you to life and which will lead you to death? God's Word is life. Follow God to live.

Prayer - Lord teach us to abide in your commandments and not the commandments and fashion of this world.

In Jesus Christ name, we pray

Amen.

Lesson 14:

The law of the wise is a fountain of life, to depart from the snares of death.

(Proverbs 13:14)

How do you know who to trust nowadays? Who do you turn to for advice and how do you know it's the right advice? It's really hard to tell and put a bead on who is real and who is really false because of the many deceptive tricks and lies a person can tell you. How do you know who to trust and who not to trust is guiding you down the right road?

The answer is...you don't! One of the first lessons of the street and or block is trust no one because all people will mislead you at some point. Who do you trust if not God, whom do you turn to when guidance is needed? Isn't that a little bit ridiculous not to trust in anybody and just consider everybody's advice who don't come from a Godly perspective or a perspective coming from experience kinda foolish?

Try to understand what I am saying. I am not at all saying that you should not believe anybody, but what I *am* saying is that you should ultimately not trust in anybody. The first and foremost thing you should trust beyond anything is God and Christ Jesus in particular.

Every other way or source is the way of death if it is does not come under the teachings and lessons of Christ Jesus or the Word of God.

As scripture says, there are traps waiting for you. As you begin to step each time, a landmine is waiting to explode right in your face. Each decision you make in life takes you down a certain road, be that road life or death.

Traps are waiting for you if you are not wise enough to "know the ledge." You will get caught by mess you didn't intend to get caught up in. That undercover cop posed as a junkie you didn't know was undercover while you were buying your drugs, somebody you "dissed" or insulted comes back the next day and starts firing off shots at you, the girl you slept with at the party a few months ago comes to find out she had HIV. Traps are waiting for you at every path and at every end.

Our scripture records that the law of the wise is a fountain of life. It's a fountain that never ceases to flow and never dries up. It will lead you always toward a path that leads to love and harmony with men so you won't have to worry about jail time or getting locked up on some gun possession charge. Following the way of God causes you to think clear and make the right choices and not to fall into the traps laid by Satan that has trapped so many others. Today's lesson teaches us to choose and walk the path that leads to life and forget the other path which only leads to traps that that lead to your death.

WISDOM for the block:

Trust no man is the main mantra of the street. This is a truth: only God do we trust to show us true wisdom and also to connect to those who can advise us further.

Prayer - I pray God that you help us choose the path of righteousness, and not the path laden with traps.

In Jesus Christ name, we pray

Amen.

Lesson 15:

Good understanding giveth favor; but the way of the transgressor is hard.

(Proverbs 13:15)

One of the best quips or sayings ever created was "Work smarter, not harder." Not to say that working hard is not smart in itself, because that is a fruit of working smart also. However the saying is stating, don't make things so complex when they are relatively simple, or don't waste your energy into one thing that can be done in a minute's time with the proper and wise approach. In our want it quick and want it now society and culture, sometimes the way that is the proper way to achieve things is not the way we particularly desire because it takes so long to get using this particular method. We want what we want quick and now, so we resort to going for the method that takes more effort to do. In turn, we wear ourselves out or destroy ourselves even more.

Jesus tells us in Matthew chapter 7:13-14, Enter at the straight gate because it is narrow and it leads to life in God but we choose the wide gate because that is easy to get through because of the space, but many men don't know that gate leads to death. While the way to true prosperity is to enter through the gate that is hard to get through. Many men have taken the easy road to success by going through the wide gate. To get cash quick many have the quick route to financial gain by engaging in enterprises that bring up the question of legality not to mention of dignity and self-respect. Of course, in this society, the best money that pays is dirty money because of people's overwhelming drive to sin and to invest in the things of sin. Whether it be on street level with gambling, drug dealing, and robbing to the corporate level with money laundering, blackmail or corporate espionage, dirty money sells and is made quicker than the honest dollar.

At the end, the almighty quest for this type of money leads to either a life behind bars or either dead in a gutter. There has never been in history to my knowledge a person who has attained wealth through illicit means and not being questioned or their empire taken down.

The one who gets his wealth through honest and dignified hard work doesn't have to worry about any of that. We all know about how the government takes big chunks our of our checks and a lot of times uses it for means that don't put it back where it should be put back, even in times of crisis. These chunks are necessary for the road construction and gas for the Maybachs and Coups or expensive cars we claim we possess. This comes from good understanding or otherwise known as common sense, which teaches the right way will lead you to less pressure and drama in your life. Choosing the right way leads you to clearer thinking over the way where you would always have to watch your back and your wealth.

Which gate will you choose? The wide gate or the narrow gate? The easy road or the hard road? Good understanding and knowledge will lead you in a way that will always make anything ventured into become easy to manage with nothing but peace as the main road to walk on. In every situation assess every situation and decide whether by God's standards will this lead toward my prosperity or toward my destruction. Then follow that road without any regrets or worries.

WISDOM for the block:

You can tell if something is under God's favor because it will either rise because it is under His protection, or fall because it is outside of it. Make sure that whatever you are doing is lined up under God's priorities and will.

Prayer - Lord give us good understanding so that we may follow nothing but Your way and Your Word, which is nothing but peace.

In Christ name we pray

Amen.

Lesson 16:

Every prudent man dealeth with knowledge, but a fool layeth open his folly.

(Proverbs 13:16)

As the old saying goes, "The definition of a fool is a person that keeps doing the same mistake over and over again." A more concise quote is by Gichin Funakoshi, founder of modern day Karate, who states, "Accidents occur because of neglect." The reason for the mistake is because knowledge is not present or neglected to make the right decision in different matters or situations. Too many times we have said or heard someone say, "Oh I could of prevented that if..." or "I should of known...." Do you know how you know who is really successful in this world? Those that do their best to stay out of the headlines of the tabloids.

Right conduct and decision does not alleviate you from the talk of others who want you to take their side and those who say you are not "Keeping it real" with the values you hold. What is reality then? Is it what somebody says that is real or is it truth that is reality itself? What is true? What is false? Pilate asked Jesus when Jesus told him He is the truth, Pilate responded to Jesus, "What is truth?" Truth is anything that is real and based on reality and not what someone says is reality especially from people who have no truth in them.

Those with knowledge can see the reality of things between what's fake and what's real. The false and real people. Knowledge of God separates fact from fiction based on the character and standards of that person. Money and power are only attractive because that is all one is blinded with. Knowledge sees it really as a man accumulating items that really amount to nothing when knowledge reveals it as so.

Today's lesson is never be afraid to follow the knowledge of God because those who follow other ways and methods will fail and their works will get blown away. It is literally the difference between those who will walk and have successful lives, and those who will end up in a pine box six feet deep. It is all in the knowledge that directs your steps toward one path or another. The knowledge of God will always direct your path toward life because Christ is life.

WISDOM for the block:

A man's decisions are ordered by his wisdom and knowledge in that area of his life. When anything is outside of God's wisdom, everything just blows up in that man's face because God is not in the equation. Put God in the mix of the knowledge that you have and you will not slip in the slightest.

Prayer - Please Lord, order our steps in Your knowledge and not in those who will fall to their own wisdom.

In Jesus Christ name, we pray

Amen.

Lesson 17:

A wicked messenger falleth into mischief, but a faithful ambassador is health.

(Proverbs 13:17)

There are two types of people in this world. Those who represent wrong, and those who represent right. The wicked ones and the faithful ones; those who bring destruction and death, and those who bring life and health. With that being said, the question that you are probably asking yourself is, "Who am I? Am I one who brings death or am I one who brings life?"

The wicked messenger's business is always to do some type of dirt or mischief. He/She is the one who is the main one who betrays trust between his compadres. He is the one to do shady side deals at his jobs to just to get more money. But in the end, he is usually found out and faces the penalty of death or jail. Since God shines light on the works of the good and evil man.

As it is obviously evident in today's society, the wicked man is running things. Or it at least seems that way. The wicked may because of their deceit and deception may own all the money and may have a significant amount of power and influence, but what is this power and influence that they possess? In the eyes of God, who is the creator and sustainer of all things, all material things unless it lifts up the name of Christ, is basically trash. Your MayBach Benz, junk, your million dollar home, trash, your gold plated Rolex or diamond watch, garbage, and especially the respect you get from others, sewage water.

That's how God sees everything that man puts his pride in for the simple fact all these things were made by human hands. The wicked puts faith in these things for his respect and image because of their appeal. To God, it's all nothing and He will bring down the wicked with his fake idolatry and the message that he is giving and promoting with this idolatry and show and prove, as scripture says, that He is the Lord.

The ones who follow the laws of God do not have any worries in this. The truly faithful have health because his word is his bond. He stands by his word. If he says he will do something, take his word that he will do it. If he says something will happen, it will happen. He is the one who tries and squashes drama or any type of conflict for the sake of the unity that scripture speaks about in Matthew 5:9.

Jesus is our model for the faithful man because in Him is faith, reconciliation, and purpose. The wicked man will always follow his own way that leads to destruction, ultimately becoming labeled as a snitch and being dealt with as a snitch accordingly, but you know how that goes. Those who follow the right path of God, and Christ in particular, will not fail in their word, and especially in their character.

The lesson we learn today do not follow a path that leads to a destructive end because people will only remember you for that after you are gone. The righteousness will have an impact where his/her words will lead to only one source, which is God.

WISDOM for the block:

What message are you delivering? Is it one to destroy or to build? Is it one to sustain or to defame? We may scoff at the killer on the street but those who give the wrong message are just as guilty; even more than those who kill. Which are you, the messenger of life or death?

Prayer - God if I am an evil messenger, please change my ways and walk and let me represent as a faithful messenger for you.

In Jesus name, we pray

Amen.

Lesson 18:

Poverty and shame shall be to him that refuseth instruction, but he that regardeth reproof shall be honoured.

(Proverbs 13:18)

"Son, turn that radio down!", "I don't want you hanging with those guys!", "Don't talk back to me!" Heard these or similar comments before? Sounds all too common, right? The constant wailing of parents or guardians can be overwhelming at times. Do you know without it and without instruction, we would follow the path down the road of being broke and disrespected?

Depending, of course, who you choose to get your respect from is an issue also, but not listening to advice that could potentially save your life one day, could lead you quicker to a jail cell or six feet deep faster than you think. Many people think that good instruction is an infringement on their liberties. It's natural for anyone to explore and try new things on their own. Sometimes through experimentation, some of the greatest discoveries were made. Benjamin Franklin would never have discovered electricity if he would have not went outside a stormy night and tied a key to a kite.

There must be an understanding. Ben calculated the risks. He just didn't go out and say, "Ok, this is going to work, no questions asked." He prepared in case something did go wrong. Many people are taking risks without thinking about the consequences afterward. Even if they know the consequences from the advice of someone who knows what's going on, they do it anyway because they feel to give into good instruction would be a violation of their rights.

"Nobody's gonna tell me what to do!" That's the attitude that has left most of our young brothers and sisters face down dead in a street or alleyway.

As scripture says, poverty and shame shall be unto him that refuseth instruction. A person is known more by their rep than their name. So, when in talk when referring to a person, that person will be referred to by what he/she did other than by their name themselves. Julie Johnson will not be known by Julie Johnson but by Julie the tease, or Julie the smart one because as the old saying goes, "Her reputation proceeded her. This is, however, the process that poverty comes. It brings shame because good instruction is refused and when good instruction is refused, then the effects of shame are sure to follow.

One, who seeks direction from the person with more wisdom in these matters, shall always stand because first they are standing on God's Word and God's Word alone. Anything else, even though it may seem like it is will fall under the feet of God's Word when put to the situation.

The Word stands against every word, insult, baseball bat, or bullet. While others who don't have the Word shall fall because of their lack of instruction, the ones who listen to instruction will rise because of their willingness to learn.

When you look at the ones who it looks like that person never has a problem, never have baby mama issues; never catching criminal cases; never in any drama; they learned somewhere or by someone by listening to stay away from all the drama by being wise by not falling into it. Even though the object is not to conduct yourself in a way so that you can look better than everyone else, people will give you respect for being the one that is not caught up in the drama that leads the average person who engages in that type of tomfoolery, severely beaten, locked up; or pushing up daisies in a cemetery.

His point in acting in this manner is not to disgrace him/her. He/she knows that leaves a skeleton in that person's character. Everyone has skeletons they are not proud of sharing, but the wise man looks back at that and doesn't follow that route again. Because of sound wisdom and instruction either from the creator Almighty Himself, or from the advice of others who follow God's Word, he/she will not fall into the trap of ignorance, poverty, and death.

Through the image of getting knowledge and wisdom from those who know more or have been in the game longer, is more beneficial than those who don't follow

God's laws and standards of living. Seek only that which brings you life and life is found in the Word of God and those who teach it.

WISDOM for the block:

What you do defines you more than what you say about yourself. Words are cheap but actions are the real truth.

Prayer - Lord help us seek out wisdom and knowledge, not only from You but those who teach Your Word also.

In Jesus Christ name, I pray.

Amen.

Lesson 19:

The desire accomplished is sweet to the soul, but it is abomination to fools to depart from evil.

(Proverbs 13:19)

Two desires run through man's veins every single day. The desire to do good and the desire to do evil. Which one you follow depends on which one you feel you get the most benefits from and which one satisfies you the most. As you have noticed in today's world, the latter is always chosen over the former.

Why is it that when you look in the news or in look in any entertainment or Hip Hop magazine, or look in the news, the ones who are usually locked up or shot usually lead lives that end up in getting them locked up or shot? Just as Satan knows his end and he is taking down as many followers as possible, the thug or person acting belligerent should know that his destruction is a straight bullet headed toward him or a long nice not so quiet stay in the prison of the judge's choice. Of course, this is the desire of those who are blind to everything except their own way which leads to the destruction they can't see.

What is it all for; for notoriety, for release, or just to impress peers? It all comes down to one thing that the world constantly looks for day in and day out, especially in our world, happiness. Can happiness give you the above or will that truly be there even after you are gone?

To know what to put your trust in is what has created kings and also brought their kingdoms down. It is the exact same thing that has brought every sinner and crime boss down from Judas who betrayed Jesus to Tony Montana in the movie Scarface who thought he ruled the world, Jesus asks the question in Matthew 16:26; "For what is a man profited, if he shall gain the whole world, and lose his own soul?" Or what shall a man give in exchange for his soul?" When one puts his eyes on the things of this world, which will pass away as fast as his/her life will, then that man's life itself can be categorized as plastic as the credit card he boasts about. Since God is life and life is God, nothing is compared or takes away from Him.

God has already created everything. Man should strive to be in Him, which does not involve just for monetary gain, which only feeds that longing for that thing that looks for the temporary. Cars will die and go out of style, the hottest girls/guys will either leave you, get tired of you, or become a total pain or nag to be around, and just like the sands of the hourglass, so goes the money in your hand. Everything bought with money will disappear because everything that is seen is temporary, nothing will remain existent that one can see, but the things that give you peace are the things that are rarely seen. You may be making some money and have a good paying job, but just one question has to be asked....are you happy?

There is nothing sweeter than striving for the things of God. There is nothing more satisfying than to be mastered by Christ Jesus and following Him every step of the way. A sense of satisfaction that you are doing something real and not fake is present when you are doing the things of God. Anything and everything else rots the soul; it makes you always worry and wonder what if what I am doing is the right thing. In legal terms, this is called "Mens Rea" or guilty mind. With God and Christ in particular on your side, there is no case of the guilty mind happening, because following the ways of God means that you will always, without question, make the right decision.

The blind and evil man can't see past the dirt or evil that he/she is doing because that's all he/she knows is just to do dirt. To do any other way is just not acceptable and does not bring happiness because the blind and evil man's passion is in doing dirt. Therefore, their love is of anything that involves sin and destruction.

Men/women who know right don't even concern themselves with doing dirt or doing evil because they know exactly where it will lead them. They know the penalty so they don't follow that route. Just know one thing, nothing is sweeter than having God's wisdom and following what it dictates and says. The whole world and all its vanity and jewelry and money may become sour but those who love wisdom don't even look twice in that direction, because there is no allurement there and most definitely no satisfaction; and most definitely a life with peace is better than a life where you have to watch your back all the time....right?

WISDOM for the block:

There is nothing sweeter than following that which brings stability and peace to your soul, and the only thing that brings that is a relationship with Christ and following God's Word.

Prayer: Lord let us always cherish the taste of righteousness and not even savor or eat the food of unrighteousness.

In Christ name, we pray

Amen.

Lesson 20:

He that walketh with wise men shall be wise: but a companion of fools shall be destroyed.

(Proverbs 13:20)

There is without question a right crew or man you should have on your side, and a wrong crew or man that you have outside your circle. The character that these person or persons show in what they do is not only due to a religious zeal, but shows that anything less is detrimental to character and image. Not getting weeded out or smoking marijuana, not drinking or smoking, and not looking at the vanity that this world shows off constantly, through images of success and sex, shows that the person who has the right mind that anything that even looks like a distraction to one's goals and dreams of what God truly ordained them to do for His glory and message should be thrown in the trash.

The reason that there are successful men or women is because they receive advice from those who know and are wise to the game that they both play. You always see both individuals talk to each other, one always advising the other in sober talk without quibbling. He is chief advisor or the "consigliere" to a good man.

You can always tell those who are real and genuine; they always get their counsel from the one who have been there first and experienced the game and can give knowledge on how life's game should be played. They get their knowledge from their true Father in heaven, so it's important to try to check if the knowledge that even the ones who have seen the truth first comes also from the truth of God.

Scripture tells us in Proverbs chapter 1:7, "The fear of the LORD is the beginning of knowledge: but fools despise wisdom and instruction." It stands to reason that those who know knowledge and true wisdom, are always speaking of God because they know that man's ways just don't work. It may work from a physical aspect and even temporarily, but from a long-term basis anything man does will not last. In street culture, it is primarily known the type of linguistic that everyone recognizes is that of the rap or "rappin" to one another. Most of the time slick proverbs are given out of this type of speech:

"Don't hate the playa, hate the game."

"If it don't make dollars, it don't make sense."

These are just some ways proverbially that communication is linguistically carried on the level of the street. Not only is it beneficial to find someone who is wise with knowledge about God and how He fits into the scheme of life, but someone who can give parable-inspired illustrations in the same tone that Jesus did.

You can always tell who has the realist crew, fellows, or associates because their crew is not full of knuckleheads or fools. Their circle is tight and organized because the people they have in their crew are known for using their heads in a situation and not their brawn, which of course, they know will lead them to prison. Stay away from any party that corresponds or parallels Proverbs chapter 1:10-14. Hanging around fools only means that you yourself by association will go down with them because everyone knows that their circle is not tight and clever, so it's easy to break a circle like that because there is nothing but a bunch of fools in that circle. You will be known by that company as also being a fool even though you may profess not to be by hanging with those who are.

When one hangs around such people, it's only just a matter of time; just a matter of time before they lose and start to act like the idiot. Just like the fools that anyone hangs with, they are going to share the same fate as the fool. When the cops pull your friends over, you may have not had the marijuana in the car with your friends but the court only sees by association that you WERE in the same car and will possibly suffer the same fate as your friends in the car by being locked up with some jail time. Those who think "wilin out" or having a crazy time is the cool thing to do are going to meet the same fate that people who "wild out" usually meet, with a .42 caliber bullet to the head, with some sexually transmitted disease, or with some very long prison time.

The lesson is, does it even pay to hang around the wicked and the fool? Of course it does, if your road leads to jail time, disease, or even death, but the way of God and Christ in particular, is that of eternal life and peace for those who want it. As far as your unity with your crew, well.... let's just say there is one partner that sticketh closer than a brother. (Proverbs 18:24).

WISDOM for the block:

To have friends or a crew around you is great, but to have friends and a crew around you *with wisdom especially from God*, is something extraordinary. Build your circle wisely.

Prayer: Please God, let my crew or circle include people who do not get me or any of my crew into anything that might lead us down a destructive path to prison or death; but always let the people I associate with have a guidance that fears nothing but God.

In Jesus Christ name, I pray

Amen.

Lesson 21:

Evil pursueth the sinners: but to the righteous good shall be repayed.

(Proverbs 13:21)

If you stand in the middle of the street in rush hour traffic, chances are you will get hit or cause destruction to other cars trying to swerve out of your direction. In any case, there will be some amount of destruction caused majorly on your part. This is the way of those who do unrighteousness and wickedness. Their way is always looking for some way to destroy spirit, soul, and body without recognition of the dangers that lie ahead. Money is the only consideration and concern when robbing a liquor store and not the thought that the store owner could have a gun. "Making love" and "Getting it in" is the only priority when two "lovers" are about to have sex and not the fact this person could have HIV or get pregnant. Having a bad boy image is always cool and a main objective to be seen as the one who is rebellious, instead of really being seen as a good guy which the one who is a "bad boy" can never ask to be because he spends so much of his time being...bad.

Destruction always follows the sinner in any way shape or form. However, there is something else that pursues them as well and that is the wrath of God and all the terrors of that wrath. It's one thing to have evil follow you which is like having a lightning bolt follow you wherever you go all over the place, but for the entity that created the lightning and the rain to destroy every plan you create and every step you plan because you fell out of favor with God is more than one can handle. Wherever they go, evil goes, and wherever they move, the bloodthirsty thugs and and goons wait to take their gold, money, and so called "ice jewelry" that they so proudly wear. They are not safe and neither should they be, because to fall out of favor with God is to be an enemy with Him and they will be dealt with as such; there will not be any place to run. This is to be believed.

Rest assured that God *will* eventually overtake them. God remember, is the creator of all the materials that man creates. He can at any moment destroy and burn up the money that one flashes while they are holding it; destroy the Maybach Benz that another flosses while they are driving it, and incinerate the outfit that one wears while they are wearing it; all the materials that man uses to make these things God has created. God according to scripture, in Romans 1:28 "gave them over to a reprobate mind, to do those things which are not convenient." Not because he is passive and sees that man is out of control, since God even can control the hearts of men just like he did Pharaoh when confronting Moses (Exodus 4:21), but because God is merciful and waits for all men to repent. Plus, it would be a worldwide bloodbath to destroy every man on the planet earth since all the items that man uses God has created. That's not God's heart. He is a God of justice and action but he is also a God of repentance and mercy and everlasting love. While the ones who think they got it like that or think they have everything under control, sleep and slumber, they don't know that destruction got their phone, cell, and house number.

The ones who walk a straight and real path, not to say their hearts don't hurt for those who do dirt or do evil, but that is the last thing on their minds, to do any type of wickedness. The righteous are not even concerned because they know that as scripture tells us in Ecclesiastes chapter 12:14 that "God shall bring every work into judgment, with every secret thing, whether it be good, or whether it be evil." The good will get what they worked so hard for after this life, and even in this life, and the evil will get their just reward on what they worked so hard for in the afterlife. The question is, will those who do dirt or do evil be ready for the reward that is going to be waiting for them on the other side? This is the big question.

All the times the righteous have been shut out of this world, from family, from crew, from friends; told their opinions are judgmental, outdated or just plain prudish. Called losers and wimps by this world and tormented for walking the straight path of purity. The one who walks a straight path who are not bothered by this world or the opinions said against them by this world can say even while in this world the words of Paul, who said Philippians 3:7, "But what things were gain to me, those I counted loss for Christ." The fame, notoriety and glamorous rock star lifestyle of this world that man tries to uplift and promote, is now trash. In the future it will still be trash and even when man reaches heaven will be trash and garbage. None that is in the world can better your soul, or being in a clique or crew cannot better your longing in your soul. The only thing that can better your soul is a man who said once "Behold old things are passed away, I make all things new." Nothing in this world to the righteous can compare to that. To the righteous, what this world promotes is utter garbage and trash and according to Jesus will be burned up like the chaff in the fire. The righteous are not concerned because vanity will meet its end, which is destruction.

As said, the righteous will be repaid for every work they have done. They know this world cannot give that because what the world gives is nothingness compared to the payment God will give. To walk a narrow and straight path may look to the one who does dirt or evil, as not exciting, entertaining and fun, but to the righteous, it's the best joy you can have living a right life, because you know while the rest of the world is going to get their reward of destruction, not only here but in the world to come, the righteous and those who are truly real can look for a reward that cannot even be measured in words, praises, or even a Benz, and that's just reality.

WISDOM for the block:

There are two ways to keep on living. You can keep on living evil or keep on living good. Difference is that trouble will always follow you and the other is that peace will always follow you. If you want peace, follow the way of God and peace will be payment for your obedience.

Prayer - God keep me on the path where righteousness will reign and rule in my life so that my reward here and in the place to come will be worthy of the hustle that you set and instructed my hand to do.

In Jesus Christ name, I pray.

Amen.

Lesson 22:

A good man leaveth an inheritance to his children's children, and the wealth of the sinner is laid up for the just.

(Proverbs 13:22)

There is one thing about the righteous man and everything he owns; if it is within the favor of God it will continue on through his children and his future seed. This of course, is because what God has blessed that man with is not for himself, but for the continuation of another generation. He does this not with a hoggish mind-set, but a mentality that was always set on being prudent, upright and frugal (a word that is foreign on the street today).

Those who have parents who carry the principles and righteousness of the Most High in their hearts, are trained in what is called stewardship or the service of giving. Through this they teach their youth to hold what they have accumulated not for a show of wealth, but for a benefit for the generation coming after will use; but mostly for the principle of teaching giving and charity, without that, the years of spending and following a frugal and prudent life would be wasted because the principle of it was not carried on to the next generation.

This is why the righteous and real man gives his substance to the Lord. He knows that he is set for the future. Man may have been setup for social security retirement fund, but how many times has the government failed in that promise of paying out? Not going against the government, which I personally love, but man's way is always setup for failure, especially when man plans it. The retirement fund that the Godly man sets up, is in the collection plate each Sunday and what service he gives to God each and every day. Not just as a door usher, which is much required as well for the greeting of guests into the house of God, but also as going out witnessing to the lost. As one pastor once said, when you enter a church, more than any responsibility you may have in that ministry, your major responsibility is of reconciliation, or bringing a man back to a relationship with God and Christ in particular.

Even if he does not leave material possessions when he passes on into heaven, he leaves instructions and a good example for the children to live by. Um, yeah, ... I think that's who the readers of this are thinking. Great, he left a good example, but I'm still broke! I was hoping dad would leave part of his inheritance so he could hook us up!

How is instruction or a Bible going to get me out of debt? I'm still broke! Scripture tells us in Proverbs 20:15 that "There is gold, and a multitude of rubies: but the lips of knowledge are a precious jewel." That is more than all the cars and mansions that your father could leave you in this world. As for the hookup, life may be a lot of things, but it is not a meal ticket. When the righteous pass away and leave an inheritance, it is not for the benefit of gaining another house. As said from the start, the reason a righteous person gives an inheritance, the real reason, is to show the act of giving and expound on that act by showing it through inheritance.

But the best part of the deal is this, not only will the wealth of the righteous be given to the children's children, but the wealth of the sinner that was included with the wealth of the righteous shall be given as well. When a man lives a righteous life, he is sure to live a long age. The wicked only lives a short span of time mostly, and has amassed a gigantic amount of wealth, which brings the question many people ask. "Why do the rich live with so much comfort, and the ones who do right live without almost any gain for living right? I mean, what's the purpose in doing right?" With saying this, just to let you know, it should not be anybody's wish for the evil or wicked man to be destroyed or die. That is not a right mindset, but scripture tells us in Deuteronomy 32:35, "their foot shall slide in due time: for the day of their calamity is at hand, and the things that shall come upon them make haste." The ones who have cars, gold, jewelry, through a system that was against God's system and for their own glory and vanity, will slip in due time and the righteous will collect their ends. Fashion companies will slip in due time and the righteous shall get all the ends they amassed and add it on to their bank.

(Job:27:17). Not because they are greedy, but because this is the order of God. The wicked die and the poor and righteous collect the ends that should have gone to poor and righteous in the first place. This is how God restores order in all things or that beautiful principle.....whatsoever a man soweth, that shall he also reap. (Galatians 6:7).

In the end, the righteous man whether through hard work or Godly living will get their rewards, get paid, and to boot, the wealth of the wicked will be added unto his wealth. God always makes it for the righteous a win-win-WIN situation.

WISDOM for the block:

Paul said in 1 Corinthians 3:22 all is yours. This is the benefit of anybody who lives a Christian life, to know that all things are yours if you live holy. God will provide even if he takes from those who don't deserve it. That is the economy of God.

Prayer: God I pray that I am good steward and a hard worker in all things and if not make me a good steward and hard worker and a follower of your Word because I know your Word says that my abundance is already set if I only follow You and your Word. Please help me follow your path, not only for myself, but so I can lay up a foundation for my future generation and seed that I will create, guide and leave an inheritance.

In Jesus Christ name, I pray

Amen.

Lesson 23:

Much food is in the tillage of the poor: but there is that is destroyed for want of judgment.

(Proverbs 13:23)

It's no surprise that there are in this world the haves and the have nots. The proletariat and the bourgeoisie, the ones who got it made and the ones who hustle just to survive; the ones who own big corporations and multimillion dollar mansions are the same people who need the labor of the ones who get paid little for their services to keep their business in check. It's amazing the number of clothes we proudly wear and don't see the alleged sweatshops and labor that goes into making one pair of jeans. What about the diamonds that we so call "ice" ourselves out with? The blood, sweat, tears and mostly blood of African laborers never see the compensation for the mining of the diamonds that we proudly and most vainly display on American and European soil.

The ones who give their blood, sweat and tears for something someone else will take credit for, they labor well. They put more blood, sweat and tears into producing that which someone else will take credit for than the man who just throws it away in a garbage can. The materials to make the BMW one "flosses" or proudly displays themselves in was made on the back of car manufacturers, mostly on the production floor that has a hand in assembling the car and are usually let go from their job at a moment's notice. These are the people that create, grind, and hustle to build the products we so proudly use without even a word of thank you to the workers who created it.

There are two words that I personally cannot stand anyone to say; these two words are as somebody scratching their nails on a chalkboard. The two words I despise anyone saying are, "I'm bored!" Just writing those two words irritates me beyond belief, but this is what you hear the rich say often, that they are bored and not only from the rich, but also from those who have little. If the rich could look out in a field and see the number of workers that toil into the night hours, the words "I'm bored" wouldn't even be a thought. You know how it goes, they can't even see that because of their shallowness as they put on their Gucci sunglasses and sigh in having nothing to do or accomplish.

Scripture tells us in Ecclesiastes 9:10, "Whatsoever thy hand findeth to do, do it with thy might." This means whatever God blessed you with as a talent, you should busy yourself with that talent. The rich neglect that and watch the poor work their talent, making the rich money while the rich sit back reclining by a poolside. The poor may have little but they will never be idle and hardly without want because they use their hands to make something happen and to make money.

Another thing to be looked at also, is not only the fact of the laziness of the rich in work ethic, but also in spirit as well. Turn on the TV nowadays and what you see from most of Hollywood's so-called stars, is the loose and wild lifestyle that is carried out. For many people who aspire to be an actor, they are looking at this saying, "You can be an actor and still come in late for shoots, or still wild out and act crazy from Monday to Sunday?" Many homes and many mansions have been lost because of the loose behavior of the rich. Scripture talks about the high-mindedness of the rich (1 Timothy 6:17), and the behavior that can befall that. Not to mention the fact that how money is not managed in the incomes of the rich.

Jermaine Dupri, the CEO of So-So Def Records, found out the hard way how when you over buy, overspend and overindulge how a fellow by the name of the IRS will come and take all that away. (by the way, he's cool now all the debts have been paid off). But men and women overbuy and max out their credit cards to purchase everything that is beyond their want... and especially their need.

In essence, while the poor may have very little according to the world standards, they have the greatest wealth according to scripture in regards to what is true wealth (James 1:9-10). Remember that just because a person is making a certain amount of wealth or amassed a certain amount of wealth, remember 90% of it is made on the backs of those who make them wealthy and have a greater discipline than the person they are making rich in terms of character. Just a few words for your mind...

WISDOM for the block:

The Bible tells us, "And having food and raiment (clothing) let us therewith be content" The basic needs of life is all we need. Anything else that we don't need is totally not necessary and outside our grasps, we need to let go because once we get those ten cars to show off, there are ten payments you have to pay for those cars which can leave you bankrupt. Be content with what God has blessed you with and roll and go with that.

Prayer: God let me not look at what man amasses as wealth and posts up at wealth but show me the true wealth as You define it and clarify it; and let me pursue that true wealth in Your Word.

In Jesus Christ name I pray

Amen.

Lesson 24:

He that spareth his rod hateth his son: but he that loveth him chasteneth him bedtimes.

(Proverbs 13:24)

"Time out, Timmy! Time out!!!" Sound familiar? "Go to your room! You are grounded for a week!" Recollecting the good ole days? Or the present day? Almost all of us have heard these sounds before from parents who were upset with something we did or what we did to our parents. These are sounds that we are too familiar with. Wrongdoing has not changed but increased. The punishment for wrongdoing has not only changed but has been eased into a form where the belt has been traded for....TIME OUT TIMMY!! There was a time where the just motion of a father reaching for his belt buckle would shut all young mouths in the house. That power has been squelched by the dialing power of 911 and reporting abuse on the part of the father.

The authority of the belt has been silenced by the politicians who now scream out abuse on the part of disciplining children through the strap. To even raise a finger to a child nowadays is instant jail time. We have replaced the honest truth of the strap with trying to "understand a child's feelings."

Since we are fallen sons of Adam and there is iniquity in us every day, there must be a constant cleansing day in and day out of our souls. Understanding quickly comes once the strap makes its appearance. The strap is the closest thing to God's rebuke that you will ever get. One lash from the strap and all debate and arguments are ended and issues are settled. Nowadays one lash from the strap lands you in court where the only arguments and issues that are being settled is whether you should have pulled the strap out in the first place.

Of course, that is often the case of parents who vent out their frustrations on their children using a strap than for discipline of the child. The purpose of the strap for the parent should never be used as a venting out tool because that child did not pay attention or do what the mother or father say do. It should be a tool used to be a physical example of what lies ahead for that child if instruction from parents are not heeded. It's better to get a lash from the father than to get it from the world being locked up in prison or catching a "beat down" from the gangs on the street for your arrogance because you didn't pay attention to your mother and father at home on how to talk and deal with people.

Train up a child in the way that he/she would go and when he is older he will not depart from it (Proverbs 22:6). Unfortunately for this society, that rule is not being enforced because now the adult is acting as wild as the child. They support the child going out to clubs and even go clubbing with the child. Teaching a son about a condom and giving them one seems to be the new birds and bees format when teaching about sex. When a society and a family encourages and gives full backing to the same thing that is destroying society, then how can we not call this a nation where we are out of control?

To obtain a stable society, there must be a certain level of control. Not for the sake of a dominating fascist dictatorship, but to show that people have a little bit of decency for their common man. **What nation would want to cooperate with another nation that doesn't share the same values as they do?** This all comes from teaching children restraint so that when older, proper conduct will be shown in any situation in life and what to do in any situation.

Oh, how a beautiful a tree is that holds a beautiful branch that when applied correctly can whip the daylights out of a morally incoherent behind that can bring about beautiful conduct out of that person.

Really, there must be a real hatred for a child not to keep them under a discipline. Even a car owner who loves his/her car would keep the oil levels at a reasonable rate. Shine it almost two times a day, check the tire levels, check the fluids and even check the lights. This is all in accordance to make sure that car is running at peak performance. Not at all or should anyone compare a human to a piece of machinery, but the same care and attention that the car owner puts into the car should be the same discipline that should be expounded on children. To have them run out in the world without a sense of respect and get shot with a .45 mm handgun because their mouth and attitude showed a lack of discernment is exactly the fruit of rebellion, because no discipline from the parent leads them down that road of death and shame.

When a child goes out into the world and does not learn discipline at home, rest assured that the gangs will show him a lesson in humility, as he is left for dead in an alleyway; or even if not so extreme, no sense of discipline or respect appears in the loss of a job because of an arrogant attitude toward the employer; or loss of relationships; friendships because of a messed up attitude that someone did not learn to control his/her temper which should have been learned at home. Notwithstanding, good parental control requires <u>good parents.</u> If the parent is living a lifestyle that is contradictory to Christ, which states in Ephesians 6:1 that parents themselves should be in the Lord, how can there be any discipline at all? All that would exist is a forged form of discipline and respect so the parent lets the child run wild and will meet his end at the hands of the one holding a double barreled shotgun if not landing him/herself in jail. Do you see now how a parent would have to have hatred for a child if he/she lets that child run into so many ills?

Is using the rod to lessen them to no more than a mule or a horse in needing of correction? Not in the least. As said in fact, if the parent does not whip the child other than

any other motive out of love to use the strap as an electric fence to teach the child of not going or doing a certain thing, then that parent would need to search his/her heart and motives because clearly that parent is not doing it
out of love but of getting out a personal frustration that the parent is going through. That should not anytime translate to the beating of a child. Then the child would REALLY have a reason to call 911!

The lesson for today is that the rod is the instrument that God has advised man to use for the instruction of young boys and young girls. It should be used accordingly in respect to reason of correction and not any other reason for that. From the strap as God has said himself, "For whom the LORD loveth he correcteth; even as a father the son in whom he delighteth." (Proverbs 3:12). So without love, whether it be in giving a beating or in heart, can we really expect anything less than children without discipline to meet their end in a destructive lifestyle?

WISDOM for the block:

If no discipline is learned at home with the strap,
then the glock or a beatdown in the street will be the rod that will discipline that young boy/girl.

Prayer - Lord I pray that through the strap corrections brought forth, not because of a wrong done but to keep a child from walking a future road of destruction. Let the parent have the right attitude and conscience when applying the strap, not out of contention but out of love for correcting the child.

In Jesus Christ name, I pray

Amen.

Lesson 25:

The righteous eateth to the satisfying of his soul: but the belly of the wicked shall want.

(Proverbs 13:25)

"Big houses, big cars, big diamond chain, that's my M.O. homee, to have everything BIG!" That is the current status of the world. Everything must be BIG! We say the term "Livin' Large" because we are living a larger than life reality consisting of everything being bigger than normal life. It's a big world and I'm owning it! "The world is yours!" thus said Al Pacino of the movie Scarface.

In the image of the American dream, it is a requirement to have everything larger than life. This is to signify that I have made it and I'm living my life like it's big and golden. I'm not settling for small change or small minds with ideas on small change. I'm only looking at those who are interested in people who have minds on, as the blues singer once said, "Big Head Money." That's what I want, that's the type of cheddah, cheese, and cake of dough and money that I want to stack. I want big dough! This is the clarion call for the streets. This is the American dream .... or illusion.

Illusion because those who are real and have knowledge know what's real know they do not need anything big.

The real know that simplicity is the key to life. Anything they need, is for an on the spot real necessity in life, and not for the show of others, and certainly not for cluttering up the house. $200 dollar shoes when a $30 or $40 dollar pair would be just as sufficient and just as strong; but again it's not the shoe, it's the brand, how it looks and how others look at you with it on.

The desires of those who really keep it real do not go beyond the boundaries of absurdity or good common sense. Their desires are always moderate and are meant to bring more production to one's lifestyle or a TRUE necessity to one's life. One rule I have always personally followed all my life is, don't spend money on things that is not going to make you money. If you are an artist, you spend money on things that an artist would spend money on to better his/her skill. Books, easels, paints, anything to build the skills of the artist and gain inspiration. What is usually spent by the average person? Shoes, clothes, rims, grills, girls. As Maulana Karenga, the creator of Kawanzaa, once said, "The buying of records cannot change the condition of your life." It can give inspiration however depending on what the artist sings, raps, or plays can give inspiration to change your life or be used to give more inspiration to the work you are currently working on, but records cannot change your life. What you do and what you stand for should matter and don't stand for that which does not bring positive changes your life.

Every living organism God takes care of. We see the pigeons on the sidewalk. They don't have to go into a store and rob the shop owner, they are satisfied with the bread they find on the sidewalk. They also find worms in the park they can pluck out of the ground. In other words, they are content within their boundaries and are happy. Today's mentality of the world is not like that. It has the mentality of, "I don't want to be eating bread and beans all my life! I want to dine on Filet Mignon!"

The reason for the want because that's what the rich are eating. Of course, I want to be where they are at. Scripture tells us in 1 Timothy 6:6, "Godliness with contentment is great gain." Not being where they are at because not saying this is the fate for all the rich, but scripture plainly tells us in James 1:11, "For the sun is no sooner risen with a burning heat, but it withereth the grass, and the flower thereof falleth, and the grace of the fashion of it perisheth: so also shall the rich man fade away in his ways." As said, not saying this will be the fate of all the rich in the world, but those who most definitely trust in their riches and those who follow their ways are headed for that possible fate.

The one thing about those who always want is just that...they always want. They are never satisfied with the little that God gives them. Their desires are fueled by what the world says, the need only to sell their product. This is the marketing strategy of the world. To say you gotta have it and show the consequences if you don't have it. From the before and after pictures in weight loss, to the commercial about increasing your ESP (Extra Sexual Perception), the world is always trying to sell you something and always making or trying to make you look like a chump if you don't buy.

The funny part is that those who want everything in the world are never satisfied with what the world gives. They always have to go past that. They want to see not only what the world can give in the natural, but what can be dominated in the spiritual.

New Age philosophies that deem to declare yourself as God, or try to bring out a Godhood, sets that person right up for being a disciple of Satan because remember that is what Satan wanted as he was cast out of heaven by a God who told him, "There is only one boss, and that's me!"

If anything, the lesson that would be for today is that God doesn't give you what you want, He gives you what you need to survive and more importantly, to be happy and content. Would you honestly admit you would have more peace paying more bills for a more expensive car just to say that you had a nice hot car? Peace at that moment is thrown out the window, as you have to work two or three jobs to pay the car note for that one car.

It's not worth it. Always be content with what God gives you because what God gives always brings peace and contentment to the spirit to the point as James chapter 1:4, "that ye may be perfect and entire, wanting nothing."

WISDOM for the block:

True contentment is being happy with what you have even if it is eating noodles from a bowl each night. Once God sees you are content with that, then He will move you up to eat even more and get more than what you have because He sees you have contentment. That is how you survive on the streets without losing your mind. Contentment.

Prayer: God let my heart be content with what You have given and the things that You continue to give. Remind me constantly they are not only for my benefit but also brings remembrance in my soul to realize that contentment is not counted in the number of things that you have, but in what you are happy with now. Let me be content in whatever state I am in at this present time.

In Jesus Christ name, we pray

Amen.

Before You Hit The Block...

There is something that is crucial that needs to be said. We acquire wisdom from a number of places, a number of people and a number of things. The best wisdom you can ever get is from Almighty God and God provides that. Through His Bible and through His Word you can conquer and master the traps Satan has prepared for the average person walking the streets today. The book of Proverbs is an incredible place to start getting wisdom.

I pray this book will be a help to you to conquer and guide you toward all truth in your life. However, there is a catch. The one who wrote the Proverbs was Solomon and Solomon prayed in I Kings 3:9 that he would be granted wisdom from God that he may lead God's people, so these words are not mine; they are not Solomon's; they are God's. Everything goes back to Him.

With that being said, one thing has to be understood and this will be said often. Proverbs 9:10 tells us that the fear of the Lord is the beginning of wisdom. Everything goes back to God and relationship to him. To use this book without a relationship to God in particular, is the same as falling in the same traps that Satan has for us because there is no guidance from God. The reason there is no guidance is there is no relationship. Solomon was the wisest man in all of Israel but he lost his kingdom

because he had women in his court who had other gods. In other words, he had other relationships with women in his court that worshiped other gods and it turned out that he soon created relationships other than God and Exodus chapter 20:3 says, "Thou shalt have no other gods before me."

The first thing before you even use God's wisdom that has to be established is correct relationship. How do you establish this relationship with God to use His wisdom in the right way? Jesus said First of all as we have just read that the fear of the Lord is the beginning of knowledge. Everything starts with recognizing that God over all and above all and demands and is worthy of worship and praise. The second way is Jesus said in John 14:6 "I am the way, the truth, and the life: no man cometh unto the Father, but by me." To come to Christ is to recognize that your are a sinner and confessing you are a sinner, turning from the dirt and evil you were doing in this world, and accepting Jesus Christ as your Lord and Savior, and start living for Him who will guide you in all truth in Him since He is the light, the truth and the way. Once you have that relationship, even though Satan will try, nothing can touch you externally or internally in these streets, because you are protected by the Most High God and you are now living a life for Him and not the world. Before you even use one jot or tittle of this wisdom, make sure your life is right with Christ Jesus, lest God brings destruction on you, no matter how much of God's wisdom you possess.

Accept His offer of salvation today because He is waiting to give you wisdom and not only give you peace without measure that the world and these streets can't give through a man, woman, alcohol bottle or a joint. He can make you a soldier to save those who are headed for damnation. If you don't know how or would like to accept His offer of salvation, there is a prayer on the next page you can pray to accept Christ offer of salvation. After that find a good bible believing church, start studying feasting and living off of the Word of God, and start living in the freedom that God has provided through His son Christ Jesus, however just know one thing, that once you give your life to Christ it will not be an easy road, it will be a constant battle in your life because just as the wisdom we discussed here, Satan will try at every turn to pull you away from the wisdom of God and back to his side, don't give in. It will be a battle for the rest of your life because you have an adversary now, but through Christ you have already won because the adversary is already defeated. All you have to do is walk in the victory of Christ Jesus and start living for Him in every aspect of your life.

The fear of the Lord is the beginning of wisdom. Begin with a relationship with God today. May God bless you all today totally and greatly.

Prayer for Salvation

Father in Jesus Christ name I come humbly as I know how and I come as a sinner in your presence. I have been a (name your sins of what you have done) and I pray you forgive me of every sin that I have done that I have known and I didn't know about and I pray you wash me clean and make me whiter than snow and that you would come into my heart. I repent from my wicked ways and I pray that you help me start living for you in everything that I do. I pray that you implant me with your knowledge, wisdom and understanding to do your will. I thank you for keeping me for all these years even when I did not even know you, and I come now asking that you would forgive me and make me a new creature in your presence and create a new heart and a right spirit within me as I ask to become a child of God and a follower of Jesus Christ. I thank you God.

In Jesus Christ name I pray.

Amen.

ABOUT THE AUTHOR

Blanton P. Hardy is a writer whose writings include stories, poetry, essays, and devotionals. He is an artist and graphic artist whose works have not only been used in print for commercial products, on websites and newsletters, in print and in Christian events as well.

Mr. Hardy is a writer, computer programmer and specialist, and artist, who holds a Bachelor Degree in Sociology and Computer Science, and a Masters Degree in Information Business Management. In addition to numerous certifications. He faithfully attends New St. James Missionary Baptist Church in Birmingham, Alabama where he has been since his youth and wherever and whenever it is possible faithfully spreading the gospel of Christ to everyone he comes in contact with.

Blanton also attends public Christian events such as the Bible Reading Marathon which he participates each year, but particularly those he meets on the street and along the way whenever the Lord leads for him to witness or opportunity to witness about the love of Christ through his talent of poetry and art especially in the youth culture of today and those in the area we know as the Hip Hop culture which he is familiar with which as scripture says in Isaiah 45:3 God has promised to "give thee the treasures of darkness, and hidden riches of secret places, that thou mayest know that I, the LORD, which call thee by thy name, am the God of Israel

ABOUT THE BOOK

The School Of Hard Knocks Life Lessons For The Block From Proverbs 13 Vol I is a timely read for believers. In this day and age wisdom comes from many places and many people. Some wisdom is good and some wisdom is bad, but how much wisdom helps you deal with certain situations in a Godly manner. The School Of Hard Knocks is a helpful guide for that.

It is presented in a way that is for the average person in any block or community or just going about their day to day life who lives in any block or community or on the street who really needs wisdom on what to do in a situation. Put in small concise bites of devotions pulling from Proverbs 13, The School Of Hard Knocks will assist you in some areas in life which can get tricky but through these Proverbs, you will be able to get the right wisdom on how to handle a certain situation, particularly that orientated toward the street level and block or community level of things.

I pray this richly blesses you and leads you into all truth God's abundant jewels of wisdom to tackle any situation you may have.

A special thanks to all who have supported the endeavors of this work as you have purchased this book. May the grace of God continue to increase your knowledge and wisdom beyond measure and begin to bless you beyond anything we can do or think.

Blanton P. Hardy

Blanton P. Hardy

www.ingramcontent.com/pod-product-compliance
Lightning Source LLC
Chambersburg PA
CBHW072022110526
44592CB00012B/1401